Peace, Beauty and Joy,
Come to the Paradise!

Serena Bella

Illustrated by

Stefan R. Sanford

ISBN 978-1-64416-633-8 (paperback)
ISBN 978-1-64416-635-2 (hardcover)
ISBN 978-1-64416-634-5 (digital)

Christian Faith Publishing, Inc.
832 Park Avenue
Meadville, PA 16335
www.christianfaithpublishing.com

Printed in the United States of America

Peace, Beauty and Joy,
Come to the Paradise!

"I will praise the LORD who counsels me; even at night my conscience instructs me. You have made known to me the path of life; you will fill me with joy in your presence, with eternal pleasures at your right hand." (Psalm 16:7, 11)

What a fantastic scripture! God is on duty all the time and doesn't miss an opportunity to get our attention. He speaks to us in his written word, spiritual gifts, night visions, day visions, words of knowledge, visual images, other people, angels and the small, still voice of the Holy Spirit. Revelation we receive is held up to the plumb line of God's word to confirm the authenticity of its source. Receiving messages are wonderful and sharing them with others is a double blessing. God speaks to provide instruction, warning, comfort, correction, and love. His guidance is essential to our spiritual growth and well-being. All scripture is solid, precious, contains pearls of wisdom, and jewels of great price—a radiant gift to us!

Once I saw the royal crown jewels of England. I was among a group of tourists walking in a single line past the exhibit. The crowns, jewelry, and other royal objects were glorious to behold! They sparkled with purity of facets, settings, and design. Flashes of color moved like flames of brilliant fire, filling our senses. To think this display of beauty had started out as plain metal and rocks. Now it was a sight never to be forgotten! God must love jewels for in Revelation we read about gems adorning the New Jerusalem yet to come. She is covered in sparkle and shine!

"The wall was made of jasper, the city of pure gold, as pure as glass. The foundations of the city walls were decorated with every kind of precious stone. First foundation was jasper, second sapphire, the third agate, the fourth emerald, the fifth onyx,

the sixth ruby, seventh chrysotile, the eighth beryl, the ninth topaz, the tenth turquoise, the eleventh jacinth, and the twelfth amethyst. The twelve gates were twelve pearls, gate made of a single pearl. The great street of the city was of gold, as pure as transparent glass." (Revelation 21:18–21)

Along the way I found myself making small changes in my home. I added candles, flowers, music, twinkle lights, and fountains. They seemed to add sparkle and shine. After a while, I called this concept peace and beauty. Later, I found peace and beauty was an atmosphere where I felt God's presence. Peace, beauty, and God's presence filled my vision. Later, joy was added to make the concept complete. As time progressed, my understanding of peace, beauty, and joy grew to include rocks on my path. These rocks were lessons designed to produce beautiful gems.

This book is a collection of vignettes from my spiritual journey that produced gems to live by. The lessons are for all of us and are organized into sections. *Dreams and Visions* shares divine instruction; *Words of Knowledge and Images of Grace* shares heavenly illumination; *Handbook Planet Earth* shares useful concepts and tools; *Musings, Ponderings, and Adventures of the Heart* shares frivolity based on his word. Paradise is God's realm.

I am grateful to Mr. C. S. Lewis for he gave us *The Chronicles of Narnia*, and in my life journey, I go there often. As the apostle Paul said, "*Not that I have already obtained all this, or have already arrived at my goal, but I press on to take hold of that for which Christ Jesus took hold of me*" (Philippians 3:12).

Please come to the paradise of peace, beauty, and joy with rocks, lessons, and gems along the way!

Serena B.

Contents

Handbook, Planet Earth

Musings, Ponderings and Adventures of the Heart

"Whatever You do, Do it all for The glory of God."

1 Corinthians 10:31

Amen. Come walk with me and let the refreshing living waters flow around, over and through you. These stories are not my own; they belong to the Lord and it is my joy to share them with you.

In my life, I have received night dreams, day visions, words of knowledge, and images of grace—information God wanted me to have. I will start the book with *Dreams and Visions* and the first significant dream given to me, Jesus, Lord of all Creation. Since God felt it was important enough to give the premier position in my education, I will do the same here. This dream was compelling and marked the fork in the road of my life.

You may very well say, "What does all this have to do with me?" Good question, I'm glad you asked it! The original children, Adam and Eve, were created in the glorious Garden of Eden under the covering of a perfect and righteous Father. They were born of him and were pure. Then the Father's adversary tempted Adam and Eve to choose his way instead. They listened, ate the forbidden fruit, disobeyed the Father, and entered into a state of rebellion. Now they were under the covering of sin, and members of the enemy's camp.

All humans are descended from Adam and Eve and have inherited their sin nature. We are all born into the enemy's camp. We all have a sin nature, even if we are "good" people. The only way out of that camp is to pledge our allegiance back to the holy and pure Father. This is exactly what the Father wants above all else. In fact, he wanted it so much he sent his only son to be *the bridge* back to him. Jesus is the narrow gate by which we enter his presence and become citizens of the garden, as we were meant to be.

We all have sinned with thought, word, and deed. No one is exempt, as it is our nature. Many of us have been hurt, disappointed, or overlooked in life. It is an unfortunate reality that people fail us in one way or another. At home, school, workplace, church, wherever, it happens. So, for now, I invite all of us to take the hurts and disappointments of life and place them off to the side for just a little while. Please read the following stories with an open mind and let the Spirit of God be your guide. I will begin with a summary of earthly and spiritual events that are the foundation for these stories.

Jesus, Ambassador of Heaven

Once there was a Father, rich and powerful beyond anything we can imagine, and he created a domain that was remarkable in every way. He spared no detail from his creation, a habitat unlike any other, and it reflected his goodness and his glory. This Father placed his crowning achievement,

children created in his own image, in this perfect garden of delight. The Father walked daily with his children and developed a relationship with them. The Father loved them and hoped they would love him too and follow his way. This was plan A.

There was a wrinkle in this perfect world, the presence of an adversary of the Father bent on defying and hurting him in any way he could. This adversary would stop at nothing to trip his beloved children and make them fall.

The Father placed a test in the garden. His children could have anything they wanted in the garden, the only thing forbidden was eating fruit from the tree of the knowledge of good and evil. The adversary saw his chance and offered a lie of temptation to the children. Alas, it was too strong for the children to resist and they bowed to the evil one and failed the test. The forbidden fruit was plucked from the tree and tasted. The children's innocence fled, and they hid from the Father when he came to the garden. The Father could see the children were no longer pure and fit to live in the beautiful paradise he had created. Sin had entered the world. Sadly, the children were cast out and barred from the entrance. Even though the adversary had won the battle, the Father still loved his children. This marked the end of Plan A.

Outside the garden, the children multiplied and populated the earth. Their sin multiplied as well. In time all memory of the garden and the loving Father were forgotten. Evil ruled the earth except for one man, named Noah, and his family.

The Father threw up his hands and said "Enough is enough, I will destroy all living people except for Noah and his family. They are the only humans worthy of life and with them we will start over." The Father instructed Noah to build an ark, which is a boat, that would withstand torrential rains and hold his family, and two of every kind of living creature, for an extended period of time. Noah followed his instructions and built the ark. This was plan B.

When the ark was ready, rain poured down from heaven and gushed up from hidden springs below. Water engulfed the earth and all its living creatures perished except the ones handpicked by the Father, asleep in the ark. In time the water receded and Noah, his family and the animals disembarked to a new landscape. The Father placed a bow of brilliant color in the sky as a sign of his promise to never again destroy mankind with water.

Starting over, however, did not solve the problem of sin. The stain of sin had been passed down to each generation and none could escape its grasp. The Father needed a different plan to rescue his children from the enemy, draw them back to himself and choose his path. To reclaim his children, he needed an ambassador. Someone who would be the face of his goodness and mercy and give his rebellious children a second chance to choose him. This was plan C.

The Father planned a daring intervention to save his children. He called out a man, Abraham and his wife Sarah, and from them created a body of people as his own. The Hebrew people would form the nation of Israel. God gave them commandments to live by, taught them about holiness, sin and forgiveness. They were instructed that the offering of innocent, sacrificial, blood was the only way to obtain forgiveness.

Later, the Hebrew children were living in captivity in Egypt. The Father wanted to free his children and gave instruction to his servant Moses. The children were to place the blood of an innocent slain lamb over their door posts before they went to sleep. That night God's judgement visited each Egyptian family with the death of first-born males. The lamb's blood placed above the Hebrew children's doors allowed the destroying angel to pass over and not harm anyone sleeping within. Through this act of judgement, the Hebrew children were given their freedom. Since then the Passover is solemnly celebrated each year with a special dinner to remember the Father's faithfulness.

At last it was time for the Father to send the perfect ambassador to be the bridge back to him. Someone who would defeat the adversary and the power of sin. The Father sent his messenger Gabriel to his hand-maiden Mary to announce his plan. She had been chosen to bring his son, the Savior, into the world. When the Father speaks, people listen and Mary agreed. Plan C came to life.

Mary, who was now married to Joseph, gave birth to the son of the Father and named him Jesus, according to the instruction given to her by the angel Gabriel. Jesus was presented to the Father on the eighth day in the temple according the culture's tradition. As Jesus grew, he went about his heavenly Father's business. He spoke with authority in the temple, surprising the elders and preparing to step into his role in history. Later as a young man, he learned his earthly father Joseph's trade of carpentry.

Finally, it was time to step into the spotlight and Jesus was baptized by his cousin John, known as John the Baptist. He entered into his Father's ministry of redemption, the purpose in coming to planet earth. Jesus called 12 men to follow him and be his disciples. He cared for the common people, healed the sick, raised the dead, spoke to the multitudes, did miracles and cleansed his father's temple. Jesus was the face and hands of his Father, and after three short years his work was almost complete. Going to Jerusalem with his disciples, Jesus entered the final and most critical stage of his life. Thursday evening, in an upper chamber, Jesus and his followers celebrated the Passover dinner. Jesus knew his hour had come and said to them, *"This is what is written: The Christ will suffer and rise from the dead on the third day, and in His name repentance and forgiveness of sins will be proclaimed to all nations, beginning in Jerusalem. You are witnesses of these things." (Luke 24:46-48)*

Jesus was loved by the people of the land, but there were wicked men who didn't want him to rock the boat of their power. They offered 30 pieces of silver to his disciple Judas to identify Jesus to the soldiers who would arrest him. After the Passover dinner, Jesus and some of his followers went to a garden to pray. Judas, the betrayer, found him there. He gave Jesus a kiss on the cheek, the sign to the soldiers, and Jesus was taken away. His wicked accusers held a trial and declared Jesus guilty and condemned him to death. Jesus was now in position to be the perfect lamb of god sent to shed his innocent blood for the sins of mankind.

On Friday morning Jesus was taken to the Roman governor, Pontius Pilate, and was presented as a criminal. He did not find Jesus to be guilty of anything that would harm his regime, but sent Jesus to Herod Antipas in Jerusalem for examination. Herod ruled Galilee as a client state of the Roman Empire and was a higher authority. Herod mocked Jesus but did not find him guilty of wrong doing.

Herod sent Jesus back to Pontius Pilate where he acquiesced and ordered Jesus to be crucified. Jesus carried his cross through the city up to Calvary hill where executions took place. There he was nailed to the cross with a sign King of the Jews above his head. He died in the afternoon before sunset and was laid to rest in a rich man's tomb. On Sunday morning his followers came to the tomb to honor him but found it empty with two angels in attendance. Jesus died on Friday and rose from the dead on Sunday, the third day, just as he had said he would!

Later, a burial cloth, called a shroud, was found with the likeness of a man who had been crucified imprinted on the linen. Known as the Shroud of Turin, it remains a mystery today. Was the image formed by the resurrection power of God? Jesus appeared to his disciples, stayed with them for forty days and encouraged them. Then he blew his breath upon them and tongues of fire appeared and danced on their heads! They received the gift of the Holy Spirit from the Father and were empowered to change the world. Then Jesus rose to heaven where he reigns, but his work is not yet finished. There are more chapters waiting to unfold. If our hearts are ready they will be exciting ones to look forward to and embrace, for Jesus will return to claim his kingdom.

Dreams and Visions

"I will praise the LORD, who counsels me;
even at night my heart instructs me.
I keep my eyes always on the LORD.
With him at my right hand, I will not be shaken."

Psalm 16:7–8

Jesus, Lord of all Creation

The day was unremarkable, and the evening without incident. Nothing happened to tip me off that I was about to meet my fate. I went to bed, fell asleep, and entered into a dream state. Not an ordinary dream but a true vision from heaven and not one to forget.

The Dream:

I was walking down a street compelled to hurry home. I didn't question it but somehow knew the importance of the occasion and I obeyed. I got to my house, entered the front door, and went into the living room. I stood in the center of the room with my back to the front wall not really sure what to do next. In a moment, I was aware that I was to turn around. I turned and faced the wall behind me that had a window that looked out onto the street. The window was eye level and rounded at the top with no glass. There framed in the window stood Jesus. THE JESUS.

Jesus was standing outside the house looking in the window at me. A divinely ordained appointment. He was completely still, yet the most dynamic and vibrant man imaginable. I observed and registered the scene to imprint on my memory to ponder and playback for years to come.

Jesus was bathed in a golden light similar to an actor on a stage standing in a dazzling floodlight. He was wearing a biblical-style robe in a light color and his body glowed from within like a pillar candle. Radiance emanated from him. His hair was shoulder length, wavy, and filled with body. Neither neat nor messy. His hair had an energy, a sparkle, and seemed to be filled with power. The hair of Jesus was not ordinary human hair.

I took all this visual information in without lingering for a moment on any detail for it did not matter. The only thing that mattered was his eyes. The eyes that see all and know all. Eyes that you can't look away from. Eyes from which there is no escape.

Jesus stood straight and tall, unblinking, staring straight into my eyes. There was no possibility of looking away from him. His eyes were captivating and without release. As his eyes looked into mine, I knew he could

see everything within me. I felt panicked and I wanted to run and hide, but I knew that was pointless and I was rooted to the spot. His penetrating eyes looked deep within me and saw things that I didn't even know were there. This search revealed my heart and soul, and I was about to get a report.

I stood there with Jesus looking into my eyes for what seemed like an eternity. I didn't know what to expect and was not prepared for what happened next. Without preamble or emotion, he spoke directly into my mind and said, "*I am disappointed in you.*" The verdict. No discussion, argument, explanation, bargaining, begging, or crying. No chance for a second chance or different judgment. It was a duet for two with only one voice. That was it, he was disappointed in me.

The dream ended and with that I awoke. What just happened? I was a believer and attended church but did not make Jesus the center of my life. I lived my life according to my own will. His words were appropriate and I knew it. Soon thereafter, I read the scripture, "*Since you call on a Father who judges each person's work impartially, live out your time as foreigners here in reverent fear*" (1 Peter 4:17).

17

God had confirmed his word to me, and I knew his vision was real. Words to ring in my ears, digest, and bring the enlightenment that he intended.

Why would God want to share his opinion of me? In the future I would realize that his eyes are on every individual, not missing a word or a thought or an action, of anyone. Nothing goes unobserved or forgotten. He knows when a bird falls to the ground and the number of hairs on our heads. God sees all the details and he doesn't grade on a class curve.

In this encounter Jesus, Lord of all Creation, was filled with controlled power and energy, there was nothing soft or loving in his countenance. He was all business. Gone was friend and companion; he was larger than life, and it was all about his plan and his purpose. In this world, we have dozens of agendas surrounding us all the time. We negotiate and get things to go our way as much as we can. If we fail, we live to fight another day. No money? No problem, there is always credit. But not when we face those eyes. The most important thing I learned is that when we face the judgement eyes of Jesus, the only thing that matters is the one standing in front of us. Not the issues that we face in our lives, only who is in our heart.

> *"For just as the Father raises the dead and gives them life, so also the Son gives life to whom He wishes. Furthermore, the Father judges no one, but has assigned all judgment to the Son, so that all may honor the Son just as they honor the Father. Whoever does not honor the Son does not honor the Father who sent Him"* (John 5:21–23). Two of the judgment scenarios of Jesus we read of in the Bible are: *"Well done, good and faithful servant! You have been faithful with a few things; I will put you in charge of many things. Come and share your master's happiness!"* (Matthew 25:21).

And, *"I never knew you. Away from me, you evildoers"* (Matthew 7:23). Now there was a third, *"I am disappointed in you."*

The bad news and the good news: *"For the wages of sin is death, but the free gift of God is eternal life in Christ Jesus our Lord"* (Romans 6:23).

"Everyone who calls on the name of the Lord will be saved" (Romans 10:13).

For it is written: *"But they will have to give account to him who is ready to judge the living and the dead" (1 Peter 4:5).*

The gems: This was a somber vision meant to bring my focus back to the crux of life on planet Earth. Who do I serve? Where will I spend eternity? I thought I knew the Lord, but did I really? This was my wake-up call and the beginning of my journey with an amazing God. Someday Jesus will sweep down from heaven on a white horse, wrap things up, and set the record straight. Our time is limited, and he is concerned that we focus on what is truly important. This message is the most startling, and brilliant, gem in the collection of the Alpha and the Omega. So, what should I do now? I felt the desire to make changes in my life but wasn't sure how to proceed. Fortunately, God had a plan.

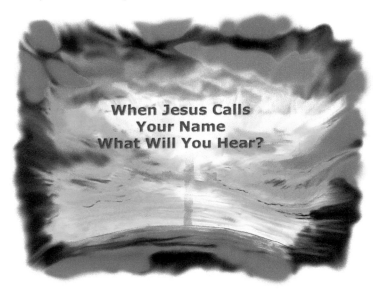

When Jesus Calls
Your Name
What Will You Hear?

Out of Darkness into Light

In the early days of being visited with inspirational dreams, I was somewhat unprepared for the experience and the message. Then as I became more comfortable with the mysteries of dream language, I began to embrace this gift. I read a book on the interpretation of dreams and felt better about trying my hand at deciphering them. God has been faithful in directing me to understand his messages.

God knows our needs before we do and starts to prepare the next step for us. At the time I had the dream of Jesus, Lord of All Creation, I was living in an apartment in a popular area of town with many worldly friends. I was involved with many secular activities but had no one to share the fellowship of my faith with. God, knowing this, provided me with a friend of a friend, who was a Christian. This lovely woman, Shining Star, was kind to me, and I hoped we could be friends.

Soon I got the opportunity to move to the area of the city where Shining Star lived. I was determined to make positive changes in my life so on that first Sunday I showed up at her church. She was warm and caring and invited me to join her and her friends! Within a few short weeks I had new friends, attended Sunday worship service and went to a midweek bible study and basically had a whole new life. This was all a welcome surprise to me, and I was very happy.

In a very short time, my life had taken a big turn. The years I spent in the company of these friends, and church leaders, laid the foundation for my future, and I will always think of this as the golden era of my spiritual life. The next dream I wish to share is one that was given to me in the early weeks of my new life. Fortunately, it was a pretty simple dream and easy to understand!

The Dream

I was alone on a mountainside that was covered with boulders and rocks; it was dusk and fast approaching dark. Rain was falling, and I was making my way down the mountain, climbing and slipping over the rocks, as there was no path to follow. As I got closer to the bottom of the slope, I saw a group of people walking toward me. I approached them and shouted to get their attention. I wanted to tell them to turn around and go back the way they came. There was no life up on the rainy dark mountain. No one in the ascending group acknowledged or spoke to me; they just kept walking up the mountain in silence until they disappeared into the darkness.

I turned and finished walking down the mountain and found myself in a wash. The wash was flat and easy to walk in, and as it continued, it got easier. Suddenly, there was a bridge overhead and as I passed under the bridge a change in the scenery took place. I stepped out into brilliant sunlight onto a white sandy beach. There was a deep blue beautiful lake and green trees. It was breathtaking! And with that the dream ended.

This is what the dream said to me: Life in the world is difficult and filled with challenges and storms. Many people cannot hear the message of God's love. They reject it and continue on an uphill journey into darkness. Somehow, I heard the call,  redirected my steps, set out down the mountain, found the path, went under the bridge, and stepped into the brilliant light of God's peace and presence. Soon I read these promises:

> *"When Jesus spoke again to the people, he said, I am the light of the world. Whoever follows me will never walk in darkness, but will have the light of life" (John 8:12).*

> *"Whoever drinks the water I give them will never thirst. Indeed, the water I give them will become in them a spring of water welling up to eternal life" (John 4:14).*

The gems: We may travel in darkness and struggle to find our own solutions. Then we find Jesus is the bridge back to our Father's presence. When we go under the bridge, Jesus becomes the covering for our sins. It is said that the two pieces of wood that formed the cross are the intersection of justice and mercy. Because of God's love, we are redeemed and are new creatures in Christ! I was elated to have a dream of affirmation that told me I was on the right track now. My new journey was just beginning!

Mirror, Mirror on the Wall

All my life I would wake up, look in the mirror, and say, "*What happened?*" Next came the getting-ready phase of the morning and the split-second timing to get out the door. Image is everything, right? I believed that for many years.

Now I had a very different life, and I was growing in new ways. I didn't know yet that when we grow in the Lord we change from the inside out. The next dream I received was a visual to give me a new perspective.

The dream was very simple. The focus was a large mirror and I was sitting in front of it, getting ready for the day. As I looked at my reflection, I saw a subtle change start to take place in the mirror. Hmm . . . This is odd, I didn't look like myself anymore. In fact, I looked really weird. My skin had become transparent and through it I could see things that shouldn't be there. Clumps of decay, different colors, it looked like I was filled with putrefying refuse from a compost heap. I was shocked and horrified at what I saw reflected in the mirror. I kept rubbing my cheek to make the ugliness go away and then I woke up.

This comment on my life was not what I was expecting, as I thought I was doing so well! So, what was the point of the dream, and what did it mean to me? Fortunately, I had friends who were on the same path of undergoing inner transformation. We had partnered together to identify areas that we needed to submit to the Lord for healing and forgiveness. I believe that however good we might look on the outside, God knows the truth. All things are new when Jesus comes into our lives on a daily, experiential level.

"But the LORD said to Samuel, 'Do not consider his appearance or his height, for I have

rejected him.' The LORD does not look at the things people look at. People look at the outward appearance, but the LORD looks at the heart" (1 Samuel 16:7).

As a group we grew, worshipped and learned to step out in faith.

> *"Therefore, if anyone is in Christ, the new creation has come: The old has gone, the new is here!"* (2 Corinthians 5:17).

Then one night, I was visited by another dream with a message from above.

The Pillar

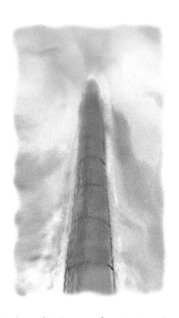

In the dream, our group was walking up a mountainside that was steep and filled with rocks, brush, and obstacles. There was no easy path up, and we didn't even know why we were doing this. Somehow it seemed to be a field trip. Suddenly, we came upon a construction zone on the hillside. It was a large site with no indication of what it would become. A palace? A temple? A hotel? A condominium? There were foundations set at different levels with floors of concrete laid down. There were no solid walls yet but posts were erected to indicate the future structure. On the second terrace was a tall pillar that went up high and seemed to vanish into the sky as though it had no end. It was a soft coral color and was in the process of being carved and shaped. There was a rough white residue covering the pillar as though it had not been polished yet. The rest of the group moved ahead on the tour, but I wanted to stay with the pillar and contemplate it. Somehow it had my attention. The group moved on for a bit then returned, and we headed back down the mountain.

I understood that as a group we were moving together in spiritual growth. I saw that we have different levels, areas both private and open. The foundation was poured and the building begun. We were each a work in progress without a marked or easy path. Our transformation process was filled with hammers, nails, and was uncomfortable at times. We were being carved and polished with the purpose of becoming vessels for God. The pillar had impacted me, and I wanted to be connected to it, but God was silent for years. Then, one day, right there in plain sight.

> *"Then our sons in their youth will be like well-nurtured plants, and our daughters will be like pillars carved to adorn a palace" (Psalm 144:12).*

It is so beautiful to think that we are being carved as pillars to be placed in a palace! Pillars are a much better statement than a compost heap! God looks upon our hearts and our outward appearance does not fool him for a minute. In his wisdom, he uses his word to reflect the truth to us. As we read, the Holy Spirit leads us into the truth we need to hear. As we follow his lead, we recognize areas within us that are being held by rebel forces then we undergo battles to reclaim the land. One of the tools that our group used to reclaim our lives was the process of inner healing. It was so easy, so powerful, and completely free! Each time we met to route the enemy, we came out victorious with an advanced position on the road to wholeness. We took our journey seriously and became a unique family. Our different backgrounds fit together like a puzzle forming a beautiful picture of diversity. Sometimes it seemed like we were a rag-tag operation but that description might have fit the first disciples, too!

> *"Do your best to present yourself to God as one approved, a worker who does not need to be ashamed and who correctly handles the word of truth" (2 Timothy 2:15).*

The gems: Growth is an uncharted territory. In the University of Planet Earth, the learning process may be a bumpy road. When you travel with The Master, you are in good company with whoever sits next to you on the bus! Trade stories, pray, praise, snooze, wake up, and do it again! We stuck with the process and made lifelong friends. The road forward only got better.

The Carpenter

Our group had been involved for several weeks in a program designed to lead us in ways to grow and share our faith. Our teacher, Mr. Equal to the Task, required a strong commitment from us to ensure we went through the course together with a united experience.

I found the course rewarding and had not missed a meeting or an opportunity to apply the steps presented to us. We had started as a group of possibly twenty-five but as the weeks stretched out the number dwindled.

I had enjoyed the material, experience, and fellowship and loved being part of this family of faith! The night before the final meeting, I had a dream. Not just any dream but a touch from the King himself!

The dream started with our group seated in an Italian restaurant to share an evening meal. Casual, red-checked tablecloths, low lighting, and happy conversation surrounded us. I was seated at the end of the long table. There were twelve of us socializing and waiting for delicious food to be served. Then I looked around at the neighboring diners, savoring the atmosphere.

As my eyes swept the room, to my right was a small table with a solitary diner. His back was near the wall, and I recognized him immediately. The light was low, but I could clearly see a man with a strong body, shoulder-length hair, plaid shirt, blue jeans, and eyes that looked right through me.

He needed no introduction, for it was Jesus. Completely caught off guard, I felt a bolt of electricity shoot through me. Then I turned to the left to clear my vision. Was this real? I saw my friends talking and laughing, oblivious to the diner on my right. Everything looked normal so I turned to see if he was still there. And he was with eyes centered on me. We continued in this moment, eyes locked together, everything else evaporating. His eyes never wavered in the dimness of the room. I didn't question his presence; I was just amazed he was there. And then Jesus spoke these words into my mind: *"I am with you always."*

That was all, the dream ended, I awoke, but the message rang in my head, loud and wonderful. This was the second time had I seen the Lord and heard his words. I was so glad the words were better than the first time. He wasn't disappointed in me now! He was with me always! Another marker event in my life, I will never be alone, always attended by THE MOST HIGH! As God said to Israel, *"So do not fear, for I am with you; do not be dismayed, for I am your God. I will strengthen you and help you; I will uphold you with my righteous right hand"* (Isaiah 41:10).

Later when I pondered this, I understood the visual. Jesus was wearing a plaid shirt and blue jeans because he was dressed as a carpenter, the profession of his time. A man who designed and built things, who put them together correctly, and was meticulous in his craft. Now he appeared in the work-clothes of the present time.

Jesus the carpenter sitting at a table-for-one in the back of a loud, dark restaurant, watching me, watching us. Speaking a message to me of his constant love and attention. I have carried this image with me daily knowing I can turn at any point and see him watching, evaluating, ready to act on my behalf. I am not anyone special. He loves each one of us like we were the only one here! Amazing!

> *"But glory, honor and peace for everyone who does good: first for the Jew, then for the Gentile. For God does not show favoritism"* (Acts 2:9–10).

The next day I went to the last session of this special bible study. I looked around and saw that our number was now twelve and somehow this seemed perfect. I shared this wonderful word from the Lord with our group and all were blessed. Amen!

The gems: We can live our lives casually, without intension. We can pass up opportunities because there is *always tomorrow*. Then we find Jesus sitting in the background, watching and observing us. He sees everything we do, hears our words, and knows the intentions of our hearts. He is with us ALWAYS! Living life more intentionally might take some practice, but with self-discipline and determination, it would be possible. Apply the Master's tools!

True North

The next story that I share is an experience I consider to be the apex, or highest point, of all my spiritual experiences. With so many amazing ways God has touched my life, this is a strong statement to make! Yet it is true, nothing can compare with this special occasion. I would love to relive it and take notes, as I should have done then, so as not to forget a single detail. But I did not do that, so now I must rely on my memory to present this most awesome story.

Our group liked to occasionally rent a house at a popular lakeside mountain resort town. So, early one spring, we booked for Friday to Sunday. It would be a special weekend because my dear friend, Joy Abounding, was moving to the opposite side of the country to start a new life with her soon-to-be husband. This would be one of our last carefree times together before her departure, and it was to be a celebration of our time together. I knew I would miss her dearly but, thankfully, was so happy for her that I could not feel sorry for myself. On Friday evening we drove up the mountain road, found the house, and settled in. Joy and I picked the downstairs bedroom to share, and we unpacked our bags. So far all was normal but that was about to change. I sat down on the bed and causally picked up my Bible and glanced at a page. I wasn't really concentrating or looking for anything in particular. I just opened the book and read a few words. Joy was in the room unpacking, talking, laughing and happy to be on vacation.

Without warning, *Wow, oh my goodness, look at this* . . . Joy stopped unpacking, walked to the side of the bed, looked at the page I was looking at, and she saw it, too. Words that were no longer words but figures, released from the page in three-dimensional form, alive and moving. Laughing, incredulous, *What is this?* Joy's sister Dawn came in to see what all the screaming was about, and we showed her the page. All she saw were flat, printed words.

"Don't you see it?"

"No. I think that the Lord is doing something that is just for the two of you." And that was our introduction to our weekend with True North.

Saturday dawned bright and beautiful, we had breakfast, cleaned up, and then headed out. Such fun and camaraderie laughing and talking as we walked along the road

that led to the village. Adventure called, and we were ready! When we arrived at the village, Joy and I decided to take a different path and separated from our friends. We walked through a large parking lot and came upon a bench placed at the edge, positioned to look out over the lake, buildings, and people. A good place to rest for a moment, breathe deeply, and savor the big, beautiful, blue outdoors.

We sat there chatting, relaxing, and happy to be alive. The sky was a big blue dome with a few scattered clouds drifting along. The lake below was a deep blue and filled with the usual activity of a tourist destination. It was an amazing and marvelous place to be! Then as we sat there we became aware that we were not alone. We sat very still, barely breathing, waiting. For what? High over our heads, lowering down over the trees and lake we could see it. A Big Blue Voluminous Robe that filled most of the sky over our heads. Looking up, it disappeared into the atmosphere. The robe swayed and moved and the edge was trimmed in something soft and white. A regal robe of righteousness worn by an invisible God so we could perceive his presence and magnificence. We held our breath . . .

As we looked up, the picture was in perspective with the robe becoming narrower and going ever upward. The breeze danced around us, the sun was warm, and we were enveloped in the experience of being present in two dimensions simultaneously. Heaven and earth. We just sat there looking up. It was just like Paul the apostle and C. S. Lewis said. The seen world is real and the unseen world is Real. All we wanted to do was remain in the glorious presence of the amazing Blue Robe. We were vaguely aware of the parking lot behind our bench and people passing by. We sat there in the real world but our senses were opened to that which we had only heard about, and read about, that which we cannot see. Thank you Lord and thank you Narnia!

Our eyes were focused above on the empty blue sky except, for us, it was not empty. It was filled with glory. If you ask me what I saw with my physical eyes, I would say nothing. If you ask me what I saw with the eyes of my heart, I would say The Father. The first

wonder was his persona, his robe, and his presence. Joy Abounding and I talked in subdued voices of reverence as we spent the day experiencing that which is invisible, yet solid in the spiritual realm. As we sat in his presence, we were complete. That is something this world can never offer. The next wonder of being in this dual state was experiencing his living words that flowed over and around us, messages that we could not articulate or take with us. Just as the words on the page of the Bible came to life, so the words flowing around us were alive.

One of the most important aspects of sitting in the King's presence was experiencing two things that we will never know in our lifetime here: majesty and holiness.

Majesty is a force that fills him, a True King. Holiness is his state of being, blazing, quiet, pure, unblemished, and complete. We shall never see true majesty or holiness in a sin-stained world. After being in the presence of true majesty and holiness, we can never be impressed or deceived by what the world presents as its version. In that dimension, one can only worship and bow down and kneel before the Lord our God, our Maker.

We never ran to catch up with our friends. We stayed rooted to our front-row seats and sat there the whole day. Only when the shadows fell did we stir and with difficulty rise and walk home. At the house we were back to reality, only really, we weren't. We couldn't explain our day and somehow our friends knew not to ask. We had been together long enough to know not to question a spiritual work in progress. Quite honestly, Joy and I didn't understand what had happened, so what could we tell anyone else?

Sunday dawned and we were on the road early, walking with purpose back to our bench at the edge of the parking lot. We wanted more of his presence and hoped that he would be there to meet us. We settled on the bench while the air was still cool and waited. We were not disappointed for, miraculously, the veil parted, and we saw again the Blue Robes approaching, coming down and stopping above the trees. We were scheduled to leave later that day and did not want to lose a moment of being in his presence. We sat there for a while and then Joy Abounding said, *"The only thing I could want now would be to depart and be with the Lord forever."* I completely agreed with her

but knew that would not be the outcome. Not yet. Joy had a wedding date, and a new life ordained by God, that waited for her.

The atmosphere suddenly changed as the time drew near to leave. The flowing robe remained as it was but then, over to our right over the lake, was a new presence. An invisible Jesus in a normal human proportion, suspended in the sky over the lake. No visual image, only a sweet presence, not regal or holy, just our wonderful friend and savior Jesus. And we marveled over this new wonder and realized that the only reason we were in the presence of the King to begin with was because of the presence of Jesus. Then just as suddenly we saw a new display further over to the right side of the lake, in front of Jesus. There in the sky were sentences streaming across the sky. Revelations, God's thoughts, revealed and uncontained. One at a time, another one starting as the last one faded away. It resembled a meteor shower or fireworks display. We laughed with delight at the spectacle. "*Look at that one! Oh, look over there!*" It was a grand finale for our time spent with the Most High!

Later that day we traveled down the mountain on our way home. It was a silent experience for me to leave the mountaintop, and the presence of the Most High, and descend into the valley of humanity. Our friends were talking and laughing on the homeward journey with no awareness of the transition between heaven and earth. I read the following passage later and felt a kinship with the apostle Paul.

> *"And I know that this man—whether in the body or apart from the body I do not know, but God knows— was caught up to paradise and heard inexpressible things, things that no one is permitted to tell"* (2 Corinthians 3, 4).

Joy Abounding and I were not caught up into paradise, but we were visited by God Most High. We were called to an audience that we never asked for and never knew we could have. We heard words that we could not take with us or share, words that were inexpressible. God's ways are the same yesterday, today and forever in how he shares his powerful presence with his children.

I resumed my life and attempted to share my experience with others but found it difficult. I didn't seem to have words that allowed others to step into the simultaneous dimensions and understand. People believed me, and were kind, but it seemed they didn't really know what to do with the information. I became silent on the subject even though, in my heart, I still saw the Blue Robes flowing over my head and words of revelation shooting across the sky. The awe never dims. Since that time, I have mused and pondered on the Majestic Holy Presence and here are some of my thoughts:

- *We all have something that we believe in and set our life values to follow.* I call it our *inner compass.* Before this event, I heard the Lord's voice and I also heard the many competing voices of the world and my own weaknesses. Now I have the Blue Robe and His Presence and this is my True North. Nothing can compete with this. I am so blessed that I have no questions regarding this truth. My compass is set.
- *This amazing God is to be known and desired above all else.* I can painfully imagine the judgment of unbelievers, people who scoffed at the idea of God, and rejected him. They will see with their own eyes the God they threw away, and it will be too late. An eternity separated from the most beautiful God of love is unthinkable, and that is the future of many.
- *Wherever God is, his court is also.* We were in his field court that weekend, such as an earthly king might have while visiting his troops. I never heard that I should take off my shoes, but I can well imagine God saying to Moses that he was standing on holy ground. *"Better is one day in his courts than a thousand elsewhere, I would rather be a doorkeeper in the house of the lord than dwell in the tents of the wicked" (Psalm 84:10).* This is my innermost heart's truth, rarely shared with others, but daily celebrated.
- *Sitting in the presence of God is a life changer.* Everything I had previously considered important in my life, such as a hobby, activity, home, relationship, or professional pursuit were not even an awareness here.

37

Looking back, I picture myself wearing a patchwork cloak. Each patch represented something that I found important. I wore the cloak to protect myself from the world's judgment and my own insecurities. With the patches, I displayed my talents, profession, life status, personality, and alliances. In the presence of God, the cloak of my identity silently slipped away. The ground opened and the cloak was gone. I didn't even notice this happening because everything the cloak represented was eclipsed by the presence of God.

- *It Is All About God.* Period. We as children think so many things are about us, our problems, our needs. God is our parent and dispenses blessings and answers to prayers as we send them up. That's his job, right? Not always, sometimes we need to be silent, wait and be open to what his plans are for us.

- This world would be a very different place if everyone received an audience with the King as we did. But alas, that is not his way, and we must continue without that benefit and instead have our audiences with the Lord in his word. Let us invite the words to speak, and perhaps they will jump off the page and dance with us in joy!

This new understanding brought changes in my heart, thoughts, and actions. Everything that I learn and experience now is with this goal in mind. Burn away the dross to become a pure vessel, shape it for the purpose he intends, glaze it so the Master can see his reflection in it, and fire it to give it strength and durability. This awareness took many years to take root and grow and gardening can be a slow process. What an amazing God, and I can't wait to see how we all turn out!

The gems: We can go through life not perceiving the magnificence of God. We may think life is all about us. Then, when we least expect it, he shows us something new. Now we know we are being transformed into his vessels. Vessels to shine for him, vessels to bring him glory.

Viewing life against the plumb line of the word is very different from viewing it against the back ground of the world. We look around and see beauty, ugly, good, and evil. We can easily become engulfed in despair. But if we step back and take another look, we just might see the Blue Robes.

"So, we fix our eyes not on what is seen, but on what is unseen, since what is seen is temporary, but what is unseen is eternal." (2 Corinthians 4:18)

The Would-Be Bride

For many years I wondered if I would ever find the love of a soul mate. I had been a flower-girl, a bridesmaid, a maid-of-honor, but never a bride. I lamented that the day would ever come that it would be me, dressed in white, walking down the aisle.

One night I had a very surprising dream about this subject. In the dream it was my wedding day, and my parents and I were at the church ready to go! As we approached the door to enter the sanctuary, the strangest realization came into my mind.
Who am I going to marry? There were no contenders in my life, so I wondered, *How can this be? What am I doing here?*

With that thought, everything went dark and I started to cry. Big inconsolable tears as I stood outside the church, ready to open the door. All was dark, and I could not take a step forward.

Then, a voice spoke to me. A voice that sounded familiar, a voice from the future. *"Don't cry, for I will be there at the appointed time."* I raised my head and the tears stopped. *What was that?* Was I hearing things? Then again, *"Don't cry, for I will be there at the appointed time."* As those words registered in my mind, I received the impression that this appointed man had brown eyes, brown hair, and was north of me. That was the end of the dream.

Marriage may not be everyone's heart's desire, but most us have something that we want. At times that special something can feel so far off, we wonder if it will ever happen. Alas, we can feel all dressed up with no place to go. Like a bride with no bridegroom.

One thing I have found is that God always has our best interests at heart. We may not recognize it, but he does have a plan. He also has a perfect time for that plan and can redirect us, as needed. God was very kind to give me a word for the future, for then I was sure that someday I would wear that white dress. Or was he just tired of me asking, *"Are we there yet?"*

I was glad to have peace, knowing that I had not been forgotten. In the meantime, God had many lessons to teach me, and my education was just getting started. One lesson learned was that the best outcomes are achieved when I hold my hopes with an open hand. Another one he revealed to me is that on the road of life I am the driver, and God is my guidance system. If I listen, he will lead me to views and back roads that will bless us both. It is a reciprocal arrangement, he leads and I listen and follow. He leads me to the destinations of his choosing, a guided tour designed for his purpose. Life is an adventure, and there are many places to visit along the way. Learning to trust God's process and timing are key elements in spiritual growth. Many seasons would pass before I met the man with the voice in my dream. When we did meet, he had a beautiful voice, brown hair, twinkling brown eyes, and lived in an area north of me. God is faithful, and I have learned to love the scripture, *"For my thoughts are not your thoughts, neither are your ways my ways, declares the LORD. As the heavens are higher than the earth, so are my ways higher than your ways and my thoughts than your thoughts"* (Isaiah 55: 8–9).

The gems: Interminable waiting accompanied by tears, disappointment, delay, confusion, and exhaustion happens. We may believe we are on a back road then realize it is actually the main road. This road gives us new points of view and perspectives. The lemons we gather on the journey makes sweet lemonade for ourselves and other travelers. Tears dried, it was time to move forward and see what the next step would be. Something wonderful, of course!

Things to Come

The future is an intriguing subject, and like many, I have spent some time wondering what is ahead for mankind. Since our world is turning ever faster, our focus can become a bit blurry. Revelation, the last book in the Bible, is part of God's handbook, Planet Earth. In it, we read about what the world will undergo before the return of Jesus. Scary stuff, but our job is to be brave, occupy, and be vigilant shining his light in the darkness. No one knows the day and the hour of the return of Jesus. For now, we know he is watching, and at the appointed time, all the prophesies will come to pass. But the question still lingered in my mind: *What is coming Lord, and when?*

One night I had a dream. I knew it was about the end times, and I was both excited and perplexed. That dream was followed in rapid succession by two more dreams on the subject. Revelation is a closed book until the end of the age, but it seemed to me that things were heating up. Now I had three dreams to ponder. A little background for this period of time is, microwave ovens had just been introduced. No cordless telephones yet, nothing from the technological era that was fast approaching. Life was still straightforward and simple, at least for me.

The First Dream:

The dream opened with a group of friends, and me, in a house. There was a kitchen and a connected living room. I was standing in the kitchen holding a large bowl stirring up a batch of chocolate chip cookies. As I stirred the cookie dough, it suddenly turned into spiderwebs. The bowl was filled with tiny fibers of webs circling the sides, and in horror, I threw it down. Then I turned back toward the living room where my friends were gathered. The walls of the room had several windows and the sun was shining in. I looked up and on the outside of one of the windows was a man standing on a ladder, looking in. I caught the man's eyes and held his gaze for a moment. He was in the process of nailing a tarp over the outside of the window. His look told me the tarp was nothing personal, it was not his idea, he was just doing his job. Then I turned, walked through the outside door and stepped into the yard. That was the end of the first dream.

The Second Dream:

My friends and I were standing outside the front doors of a large church. We had the knowledge that inside the church were kneelers, padded risers for the purpose of kneeling during the worship service. We stood at the entrance of the church and entreated the parishioners not to go into the service. We somehow knew that anyone who knelt on the risers during the service would be electrocuted. A jolt of electricity would be delivered through the kneelers, killing those who touched them. As we presented this to the people who came to the doors, we were rejected. We were sad our pleas fell on deaf ears, and we knew that all the people who entered the church would never leave it alive. That was the end of the second dream.

The Third Dream:

It was a sunny afternoon, and I was in a restaurant. I left the building and walked out to the parking lot. Then I remembered I had forgotten something and turned to go back inside and retrieve it. I turned back, walked through the doors of the restaurant, and saw a glass wall at the side of the room with a crowd of people gathered in front of it. They were focused on looking out the window, and I joined them to see what was going on. I was looking down on a very dark beach in the midst of a storm. On the beach were large rocks and boulders, crashing waves, and extreme turmoil. I had never seen such a scene of devastation. Then out of the darkness emerged three separate geysers from between the boulders. Three red geysers of blood gushing high into the air. We all stood silently at the window and watched the black turmoil. That was the end of the third dream.

This was quite unusual for me, to be given three dreams in short succession with messages of the future. I knew that God was never wrong, and he always keeps his word. I believed he would reveal the meaning of the dreams to me in his time. Here are my thoughts.

Dream one: I puzzled over the chocolate chip dough and spiderwebs for years. Then, as we moved into the technological age, it made sense. The cookie dough represented a sweeter, simpler time of life. The spiderwebs in the round bowl, aka globe, were the new era of the World Wide Web. The world changed quickly from sweet to intertwined and connected. Next a man placed a tarp over the window. He was a tech-guy, putting up a tarp, or restrictions, on our group as Christians to keep us in the dark. A blackout of information. It was not personal; he was just doing his job.

Dream two: There are two scenarios for this dream. The purpose of the church could have been for the worshipping of Jesus, and with the antichrist in power, the consequence would be death. Or, it could have been people going to worship the antichrist, and the consequence of that would be eternal death. It seems Christians would see, and be affected by, these end-time events.

Dream three: It was a beautiful day with no hint of a disastrous storm approaching. I was happy, comfortable, walking in safety, and enjoying the afternoon. Without a jolt or a wrinkle, I was suddenly in a heavenly vault looking down on the destruction of my earthly home. How does one make that transition? Either I died and went to heaven, or I was raptured into heaven. A few days after I had this dream, Gentle Friend and I were having dinner at a restaurant on the coast. We had a table by the window and it was dark outside. Beneath us was a beach with boulders and rocks. Waves crashed against them with violence and force. The scene was eerily familiar. *Did God just confirm the third dream to me?* I felt he had.

Looking at the dream, it seems that devastation may be coming on the earth in the twinkling of an eye. Christians may also be airlifted out of harm's way in the twinkling of an eye. I believe that when we place our faith in Jesus, we will dwell with him in the light forever. Without that decision, darkness will prevail and consume. The meaning of these dreams will become clearer through time and events, and my opinions may change. For now, my thought is that God, our loving father, will rescue his children from experiencing the main body of his wrath, which is meant to punish an unregenerate world. *"For behold, I create new heavens and a new earth; And the former things will not be remembered or come to mind"* *(Isaiah 65:17).*

The gems: Our lives can feel uncertain, but the word says that God walks with us in the storms of life and his plan will prevail over all. He is with us always, even unto the end of the age and he has given us promises to look forward to. Lord, please give us your grace and your strength to face the future!

"Blessed is the man who perseveres under trial, because when he has stood the test, he will receive the crown of life that God has promised to those who love Him" (James 1:12).

The Sheepdog

The following is a magnificent dream with a vision for my future. It was, by far, the longest, most complex of all the dreams given to me. I do not know why God chooses to give me dreams, but they must serve his purpose. *Learning to trust him for the future, perhaps?*

Part One—My Life:

It was night, and I was driving on a narrow road through a wooded area. Ahead of me was a house standing by itself. The house was built from wood and had  many windows that gleamed with light. I entered the house and stepped into the living room. There were many people that I seemed to know, and the atmosphere was happy. I looked around the room and then looked up toward the ceiling. Slightly below the crown molding hung portraits of people. They lined the tops of the walls and each one was of an individual with a price tag attached to it. After taking this all in, I wanted to see the rest of the house. In the center of the back wall was a door leading to the inner part of the house. I knew I was allowed to go there and opened the door. As I stepped through, I immediately entered the private part of the house. There was no party there, only four men in brown suits who stepped up to escort me on my tour. There was a short hall on my left side, and I turned and walked down it. At the end of the hall was an archway and a room beyond it opening off the left side. I could not see into the room, but I knew my father was in there. As I got closer another man in a brown suit stepped out from the recess behind the archway. He stood in the center to bar my way.

The four men in brown suits behind me stepped forward to explain my presence. *She is the heir. She is the one to whom this belongs.* The new guard stepped back, offered his apologizes, and motioned me to enter the inner sanctum. I knew I  belonged there, I knew I had complete access to the inner room with my father, but I changed my mind and instead backed away. *Not to worry. I don't need to go in there right now. All is well.*

I turned and walked in another direction with the four brown-suited men in tow. Next I entered a round room with no furnishings except for carpet. Suddenly I was overtaken with sleepiness and dropped to the floor to take a nap. After a while, I woke up. I was alone and stood up and looked around. At the far side of the room was a door. I walked through the door and found a kitchen. The path through the kitchen was narrow, and I walked down it quickly to a door that led to the outside. The inside door was standing open and there was a screen door on the outside that I pushed through. I found myself standing on a porch that extended across the back of the farm-style house. The scene before me was beautiful.

Part Two—My Future:

Dawn was breaking and shafts of sunlight found their way through dark green trees that surrounded a field before me. The field was rough, uncultivated, and filled with dew-covered shrubs. There was a wooden fence encircling the field, and there were several brown horses at the far end of it. I knew these horses had a job to do and were about to begin their day. The beauty of the scene conveyed the feeling of being in another world and I felt I was a silent intruder. Off to the right side of the field, in the group of horses, I noticed something else. Another horse, if you could call him that. This new horse was brown like the other horses, but that's where the resemblance ended.

This new horse, even though part of the herd, was different. He didn't look like a real horse, but rather like a man in a horse's costume. This puzzled me, and I continued to look at this "odd horse." Then the horse turned his head and looked at me. Our eyes met, he broke away from the herd and started running toward me. I was startled and thought how strange this was and decided to look away and see what the rest of the field was doing. Maybe the horse would disappear.

It was now midday in the field with the sun high overhead. Several men were with the horses and they were occupied with their work. All was bright and sunny, and I felt reassured to see the calm field. Then I remembered the odd horse and looked again to my right to see if he was still there. He was there, running very fast toward me, and was much closer now. What made this even odder was that now I could see the horse wasn't a horse anymore. He was going through a transformation process. As he ran, his body was changing.

I had never seen anything like this, and it was so unbelievable I couldn't look away. Then suddenly he was in front of me, running up the steps and onto the porch. He bounded up to me, stood upright, put his paws on my shoulders, and licked my cheek. He had become an Old English Sheepdog. The odd horse had transformed into a real sheepdog. That was the end of the dream.

As you can probably imagine, my head was spinning with the images of this dream! I knew I had received an amazing touch from God and that he would explain it to me in due time. The first part of the dream was a general statement. The darkness of the night allowed the windows of the house to shine brightly as I approached. We begin our lives in darkness. When Jesus comes into our hearts, we are filled with the light of God, and he is a lamp unto our feet. We no longer blend with the night but shine and are beacons of light to others. Inside the house were portraits of people hung close to the ceiling with price tags on them. These represented that we are individuals bought with a price. When we are redeemed, we are lifted up and placed close to the heart of God. The people in the main room represented the fellowship of believers.

A door led into the private area of the house, and I went through it. I left the general area and entered my own personal space of discovery. I was given four angel escorts, and my father was close by and accessible. It was established that I was the heir to this house, or the kingdom, that I found myself in.

I continued with the exploration, but then suddenly was too tired to go on. I entered a round room with no windows or furniture. Just one door in, and one door out. I lay down and went to sleep. I believe this represented that I was called to withdraw to a secret place to continue forming like a baby in the womb. The word God gave me for this part of the dream was *dormant*. I was dormant even though, in reality, I was thriving and living an active life. This seemed contradictory to me, but that is how God saw it. When this nap had accomplished its purpose, God woke me up, and off I went out of the room. No angel escorts with me now. Walking down the narrow hall and through the kitchen was similar to a baby's birth into the world.

The first part of the dream started at night. The house was modern, made out of wood and glass, light shone brightly from the windows, and it was situated in the woods. In contrast, the second part of the dream started with a farmhouse at the dawn of a new day.

Night was vanishing as streaks of light illuminated the sky. I stood on the porch, not called to participate in any way. Just observe the beauty of the morning and watch a story unfold.

Out on the porch, I saw a shining vision of a field. I was not called to enter the field, only be a silent spectator. I watched real horses in the field. They represented real Christians who work in the fields of the world to reap the harvest. In their midst, off to the side, was an odd horse. He had joined them but was not really one of them. This odd horse saw me and recognized me as someone he wanted to join. In the process of approaching me, he underwent a transformation. The process was confusing to watch and the "horse" became unrecognizable. By the time he reached my side, he had become a new creature. I was stunned at the supernatural event I had witnessed and was presented with.

The vision of the sheepdog was ever-present in my mind for many years, just waiting, waiting, waiting. Then one day I was introduced to a man, through a friend, who went to a neighboring church. He was nice and I enjoyed him, but soon realized he was not the mature Christian man I had hoped to meet. In my opinion, he needed some serious Christian growth as he had some odd ideas. After a while I felt discouraged and stopped seeing him. A couple of months later, he turned up at my door again. He seemed sincere, we laughed, so I started dating him again. *Was this the one, an odd Christian who was going through changes to be with me?* Plus, he had an Old English Sheepdog at home! Coincidence? My mom reminded me that Rome wasn't built in a day and be patient. I could see progress in his spiritual development, but I didn't think we were really a match. I was ready to move on and then God spoke to me,

Who are you to criticize my gift? If I say he's good enough, then he's good enough. And besides, I'm not finished with him yet.

My heavenly father had arranged a marriage for me, and I confidently entered into it knowing that it was his plan and would be blessed! God was right and, as promised, my husband matured into an amazing believer, on duty, and devoted to the Shepherd.

The gems: Partnering with God for his plan can be an unpredictable journey. It can stretch us in directions that are uncomfortable and require more faith than we have. Thankfully, God is never finished with us and his blessings can come wrapped in odd packages. His timing is perfect, our faith grows, and it is all for his glory!

O ye of little faith, just look at him now!

Words of Knowledge,
Images of Grace

"For to one is given by the Spirit the word of wisdom:
To another the word of knowledge by the same Spirit."

1 Corinthians 12:8

A Starry Night

 I grew up in a small town high in the mountains where the night sky was dark and millions of stars shone brightly. I was introduced to star-gazing early, as my father's passion and profession was astronomy. My earliest memories were of being held up to a telescope and looking at the moon which was enormous, bright and filled with craters. Later, as I grew up, sitting under a nighttime canopy of sparkling stars recharged my batteries.

 One evening, I had a very different experience. It was a warm summer night and I, as per my ritual, went out to the front yard and lay down on the grass. Staring up into the sky, it was as spectacular as usual. Satellites moved slowly overhead, shooting stars zoomed by, and the grass prickled under my back. All was well, and then suddenly it wasn't. Without warning, the sky looked threatening, and I thought, what *if gravity fails and we all float away up into the dark sky? Drift into oblivion?* What was going on? It wasn't like me to have fearful thoughts about the night sky, but here I was in a panic feeling small, insignificant and insecure. Then, before those thoughts could grow and immobilize me further, another voice spoke:

> *"I placed the stars in the heavens to fill the expanse with dimension. A dome of lights overhead so you would feel secure. A night sky to encompass the earth with soft points of light and a moon to push back the darkness. My handiwork that declares my presence, even in the dark."*

A loving father making sure his kids felt safe and secure in the night. My fear vanished instantly, and I marveled that now, instead of a big, scary universe, I had a special ceiling with a giant night-light! This was good news for me, and I laughed at the thought of my silly panic! What was I thinking? Having a lie revealed and put in its proper perspective by a heavenly source was exactly what I needed. When under the influence of fear, I could not see beyond the adrenaline. That evening became imprinted on my memory, and lucky for me! How wonderful to have a father who knows when to intervene and when to stand back. As it turns out, I have often been the target of idle fears who love to come knocking. That example showed me I didn't have to listen to their nonsense. Idle fears are bullies who evaporate at the first sign of resistance. Now I just say, *"This is the day that the Lord has made and I will rejoice and be glad in it! I can't hear you idle fears, so you can just move on down the line!"* This has gone a long way in stopping a lie from distracting me and tangling my feet in a snare of deception. I once read that *"Faith is fear that has said its prayers."* I believe it! I recommend this to anyone, for *"Even the darkness will not be dark*

to you; the night will shine like the day, for darkness is as light to you" (Psalm 139:12).

The gems: Sometimes we can feel alone and frightened. God sits with us in the dark and brings us his comfort, the light of his word, which is a lamp unto our feet. He may also give us a night-light in the sky!

This was my first experience of hearing God speak to me, and it felt very natural. After I moved to the city, the black velvet sky of lights was a beautiful memory to reflect on. I will never forget how God changed my perception with those words of comfort! Thank you!

The Cross

The Cross is a story written by my
mother, Nonie, to her family. Because my
mom had wonderful encounters with
the Lord, I understood their value and
later embraced my own experiences.
This story is special, and I precede it
with some background information
to set the scene.

When I was nine years old, my
mother had a "nervous breakdown" and was
diagnosed with manic-depressive disorder.
Mental illness is a scourge for both the person,
their family, and loved ones. If you have lived with
it, you know. After this event, our family took life one
day at a time and hoped my mom would get better.
When I was twelve years old, our family moved to a nearby small
town, settled in, and looked for a new church to join. We found
a lovely small church, regularly attended services, Sunday school,
church events, and at the age of fourteen, I was confirmed into the
faith. It was our family tradition.

One day my mom was watering the neighbor's yard while
they were on vacation. She told me that on that day she was feeling
particularly depressed and hopeless, as medical treatment was not
alleviating her misery. On that day, unexpectedly and miraculously,
while sitting there with the hose in her hand, she was visited by the
Lord. She was filled with the Holy Spirit and started speaking in
tongues! Immediately, her depression lifted and the medication she
was taking began to work. My mom was elated and told everyone
about her miracle healing, and she was on fire for the Lord! When
she shared this wonderful news with the pastor and elders of our
church, they were not happy. They did not know what to do with
this information, about being born-again, and preferred she keep

it to herself. My mom could not understand this reaction and was not one to keep quiet about such wonderful news. Eventually, she left this church and years later, it was vandalized. The crime was published in the local newspaper along with a photo which she refers to in her opening statement. Nonie wrote this letter to her family to share God's blessing.

Dear Family,

I would like to share with you the story behind the mangled cross shown in the enclosed newspaper clipping. About 17 years ago, while I was still a member of this church that was so totally vandalized, I designed and helped to build the cross that hung above the alter.

A man from the congregation constructed the light-colored wooden part and I made the colored glass insert for the center of the cross. My husband had the brass-work done and the electrical part put together. I took chunks of clear red, orange and yellow glass and imbedded them in clear plastic to form a small cross placed within the wooden cross. A small, sharp pointed brass cross was placed in front of the glass cross. It represented the nails and thorns Christ suffered at his crucifixion. We finished and assembled it, then mounted it over the alter of the church with a light behind the glass area. The cross was very beautiful, graceful and colorful.

I had only been a true, or born-again Christian, for about six years when I came down with a flu-type illness. However, I attended church and taught my Sunday School class as usual the last Sunday I was there. As I sat in the pew feeling so sick and miserable the Lord, by his Holy Spirit, communicated to me that this would be the last Sunday I would ever be there to worship and He wanted me to know the significance of the colors that I had chosen to use in the cross. I had no idea that there was any significance. I thought only that I had chosen to use colors that I liked and were harmonious! Sitting there looking at the cross the colors swam and blurred through the tears that filled my eyes as the Lord said:

The red stands for my blood with which I purchased my kingdom of regenerated believers in Christ; the orange stands for the fire of the Holy Spirit which is my power; the yellow stands for the light which is my glory.

I felt so awed and thrilled to have this all revealed to me by the Lord himself! For several months following that Sunday I was confined to my home as a shut-in. I had tests done in the hospital but they did not give any answers for my extreme weakness. During this time the Lord allowed me to learn many things and one was that he wanted to lead me elsewhere to worship and serve him. Then a friend invited me to visit her church where the pastor anointed me with oil and prayed for me and Jesus healed and set me free!

It was now God's time to lead me to a congregation of believers where I could feed on the word of God and drink the water of life. I was like a spiritually starved and dehydrated sheep that had finally discovered an oasis or banquet where I belonged. My wonderful shepherd had led me!

Eventually I resigned my membership from my previous church and followed the Holy Spirit's leading to this new church of blessing. Here there was an abundance of Bible teaching and wonderful opportunities to learn and serve the Lord. Since that time I have seen God's purpose unfold in my life, and in numerous other lives as well, as a direct result of my obedience to his leading, Praise the Lord!

"Is anyone among you sick? Let them call the elders of the church to pray over them and anoint them with oil in the name of the Lord" (James 5:14).

The gems: Illness happens, rejection happens, hurt happens. Follow the spirit wherever it leads. We will have remarkable encounters with the Lord as a result of trusting him and walking in faith. He is our healer and will never leave us, nor forsake us. Thank you, Nonie, for sharing this with us. We are the richer for your faithfulness!

Simple Prayers, Faithful God

Life isn't always easy, especially when one is ill. Many people go through life with poor health or debilitating physical, mental, or emotional conditions. Sometimes the illness is on the inside, and doesn't show on the outside. Many things can take a toll on our  energy, and we can appear normal when in reality we are disabled. It can really be hard to keep believing, professing our faith, and maintaining a positive attitude when our bodies are dragging. Often just lying down and giving up seems like a better and more honest option. Maybe I just need more negative ions from the ocean?

I know about this because I have spent a lot of time being sick and tired with no obvious medical answers. Miracle healings are just that, and miracles don't happen often enough. I want you to know that I believe in miracles, I have received miracles, and I *depend* on miracles. I have also spent many silent years, just waiting. Knock, knock, anybody home up there?

To date, I have not found a way to move the hand of God according to my plan. But I will share some touches from heaven I have received, and I hope they will encourage you, especially if you are *waiting*.

I have heard it said that to get over one's own difficulties one should walk a mile in the shoes of another. That walk will usually have us counting our blessings instead of our miseries. Blisters and callouses are the result of living in a fallen world, and having compassion for others, and ourselves, should be the order of the day. Stay supportive, encouraging, and we shall overcome!

A long time ago, I had an assortment of physical maladies. One in particular seemed to drag on and on. Every day I went to work and pretended that all was well. During the week, my Bible study friends would pray for my healing to no avail. Nada, zip, goose egg. That did not stop us from praying, but nonetheless, I was discouraged.

At this time, I met my dear friend Erika who was also in our Bible study. We had things in common, laughed, and formed a bond. One day she invited me to join her, and her family, for dinner. Great, I gladly accepted and enjoyed the gracious family environment. Erika's mother, Millie, had made a delicious meal, and we all sat down to the table to enjoy it. Her father, Mr. Russell, said a simple blessing over the food. In that prayer, he included a brief sentence, "Please heal Serena and restore her to fullness of health." I sat at the table hearing this and inwardly scoffed at the petition. My friends had prayed for me so many times, why bother now? I felt irritated as I knew nothing would happen . . .

But then it did. In that moment, I knew I was healed. Wow, really? What do I do now? What do I say? I didn't do anything, didn't say a word, I just sat there and ate dinner. A few days later, I went to my doctor and after some tests he pronounced me healed, 100 percent, and didn't we do a great job! Yes, thank you very much, see you later!

I rejoiced and with enthusiasm announced to my friends the miracle healing I had received. It was so amazing to be in the well zone for a change! But wasn't it unusual to be healed when I was actually scoffing at the request, and having no faith, for the miracle asked for?

Clearly, there was a message here, and I pondered it for a long time. I believe God was teaching me: *"Grieve, mourn and wail. Change your laughter to mourning and your joy to gloom. Humble yourselves before the Lord, and he will lift you up" (James 4:9–10).* It surely had nothing to do with me. Only God answering the prayer of a man who listened to his prompting and then acted on it for his glory. It was God's timing.

At this time, there was a lot of conversation about the concepts of *"name it and claim it," "there's a miracle in your mouth,"* etc. I read some books on the subject and listened to the arguments for them. I even tried them out, but somehow they fell away. Now, with this healing, I definitely believed in his plan, his purpose, his timing.

I believe that humility is the key to our requests. Submit *the list* and hold it with an open hand. Watch and see what happens.

A few years later, my friend Erika married and moved to a neighboring state. Her parents, Millie and Mr. Russell, moved to be near her, and we kept in touch with letters. I visited her a few times and was happy that she was established with family and friends. All was well except that she wanted a baby. Time passed, and still, no beautiful, bouncing baby. One day, Mr. Russell had some health issues that required surgery. He underwent the recommended procedure and sadly did not survive. Later Erika shared with me that in that hour of grief she whispered a prayer to her departing father, *Dad, can you please ask Jesus to give me a baby?*

Almost immediately a beautiful baby was on the way! Did Mr. Russell intercede again? We only know that God is faithful to hear our prayers, and perhaps it was his timing to bring a blessing that would soften their sorrow.

Naturally, we were all happy for Erika and eagerly awaited the arrival of her long-awaited baby! One night during her pregnancy, she attended a service at her church. There was a guest speaker who had the spiritual gift of Words of Knowledge. At the end of the service, she spoke out a few anointed words for individuals in the congregation. Erika sat there listening and then the speaker turned, faced her, and said, *"You will have a son - He is a prince and wears a crown. He is of me and I have given him to you."* What an unusual prophesy to be blessed with! She pondered this in her heart and in due time gave birth to a son. The beautiful, bouncing baby boy was a delight to all our hearts! In no time at all, Crowned One was growing up, learning his lessons, drawing, painting, and aligning his heart with the Lord.

Somewhere along the way, I got married and wanted to start a family, too. It all sounded so easy, but in the end, it wasn't. After eight years, my husband and I adopted a b e a u t i f u l , bouncing baby boy! Erika was God-Mother to our son, Steady Boy, and her son was his God-Brother. It was a match made in heaven!

God continued working out his plans in our lives. Crowned One developed his artistic talent, and I was introduced to the concept of peace, beauty, and joy. God gave me stories about rocks and gems in my life, and I wanted beautiful pictures to be part of the collection. God's plan and timing were perfect and soon Crowned One was called to be the illustrator.

As I look back, I see that Mr. Russell impacted my life over many years. He prayed for my healing, and that came to pass. My friend appealed to him to intercede for a baby, and that came to pass. I needed an illustrator and his grandson appeared. Thank you very much, Mr. Russell!

The gems: We can become discouraged because our prayers don't get answered. But God does hear the prayer of a righteous person, and they are powerful and effective. He acts on our behalf, sees the big picture, and is not in a hurry. He wants things to be done right, according to his long-term plan. In God's timing, the details of the puzzle will emerge and reveal how the pieces fit together, for his purpose and glory. This puzzle turned out to be quite lovely!

The Last Dance

Death. Now here's a subject we like to avoid! I bring this up because sometimes we just need to talk about it. Sometimes, we just need to cry and carry on.

The Last Farewell Dance touches all our lives from minimal discomfort to extreme loss and pain. Sooner or later, each of us will look up and see the Dark Spector approach. As it gets closer, we turn to run and hide, but alas, it taps us on the shoulder and bids us to enter the dance floor. We stand up, take the hand of our loved one, and the dance begins. As the dance progresses, we lend our love, comfort, and support. We beg, pray, and feel helpless. What can we do? The dance can be short or long, but we know it will end at the door to eternity. This story is not meant to be sad, although many tears were shed, then and now. I share it because I have learned lessons, and received blessings, in dark corridors.

Once, long ago, I had a friend a few years older than me. He taught me things about life, and it was my first experience of having a mentor-friend. Funny, talented, particular and troubled would describe my friend. Mr. Particular had a method for doing everything and soon I was following in his footsteps. "There is a right way, and a wrong way, to do anything. You just have to decide which way you want to take." My friend also had bouts of depression and told me that someday he would end his life, and I should not feel responsible when that happened. Strange words to hear, and I felt the tap on my shoulder that started the waltz, long before the music started. Three years later, Mr. Particular lived up to his vow and was gone with no good-bye. An intentional death carries with it special sorrow and questions. What more could I have done? What did I miss, where did I fail? Depression is devastating, speaking from my own personal experience. My mother's long-term illness, and my own intermittent bouts with it along the road of life, taught me depression is not to be reasoned with. My friend coped with depression as long as he could and then made his choice.

Anyone who has lost someone unexpectedly can tell you the shock of it. Whether they are young, old, or in the prime of life, there are no words to help process this sudden and extreme loss. This was my first experience with losing a close loved one other than elderly grandparents. Outwardly, I adjusted, accepted, and went forward with my life. Inwardly, I found there was no fast track for the grieving process. There was an empty place in my heart that I filled with tears whenever sadness washed over me. This went on for several years, and I didn't seem to be any closer to finding peace with this loss.

Then one night, I had a dream. In the dream, I was walking down a sidewalk in a residential area. I turned to the left and started down a path that led to the front door of a house. As I walked toward the house, a strong wind came up and pushed against me, causing me to stay in place. I could not advance and reach the house and the dream ended.

I knew God had given me a message and soon he revealed what it meant. The Holy Spirit, manifested as a mighty wind, came up and held me back preventing me from going into the House of Mourning at the end of the path. The time had come to heal. At the next gathering of my friends, I shared this dream with them, and they laid hands on me and prayed for this empty place in my heart to be healed. As unusual as it may seem, I never again cried and grieved for my lost friend in an inconsolable manner. The black hole was gone, and I was grateful to God for his loving, healing touch.

I still missed my friend, but the loss was in a much better perspective now. What a gracious father to have taken this burden from me! There would be more taps on my shoulder, more hands to hold and more waltzes to endure. Never easy, always hard to say

has reached its earthly limit and the next stop is paradise.

The next dance I was called to attend was that of my mother, Nonie. My beautiful mother, child of god, evangelist, my first example of unconditional love. When I was little and naughty my mom would tell me, *"I don't always like you, but I always love you."* Words of wisdom for me. Nonie had been ill off and on for many years with manic-depression disorder. Nonie had experienced good years and hard years and one year when I visited my parents at Christmas, it was clear it would be her last.

Three weeks later, in January, I got the call. Not the one in the middle of the night that we all dread, but one during the day, calm and composed, informing me it was time to return to my parents' home. I booked the flight, knowing and afraid of what waited for me. When I was there at Christmas my mom was up and functioning but visibly disturbed, rocking back and forth in her chair, moaning low with her head in her hands. The pain of depression goes deep, and I hoped her departure would be easy and her soul set free. I knew it was time for her to step into the light of peace, beauty and eternity.

My lovely sister-cousins Joyous One and Merry Artiste met me at the airport with hugs and tears. I arrived at my parents' house to find a hospital bed in the living room and hospice ladies attending my mom. Not knowing what to do in this foreign situation, I sat with my mom and tried to acclimate. Nonie was past conversation so, not knowing if she was in discomfort but thought she might be, I ordered some medicine to dull any possible pain. Fortunately, there were no words left unspoken, no regrets, and my mom knew I loved her. I accepted that this was God's timing for Nonie to be taken home, and I was ready for my assignment.

Never in my wildest dreams did I ever think I would be on a life watch, sitting near a loved one, watching and waiting for their spirit to enter eternity. Well, that lasted for about ten minutes and then I needed something to do. My cousins came over, and before you knew it, we were laughing and chatting with my mom lying in the bed next to us. She became restless and didn't seem to appreciate our levity, so we moved to another room.

Later that night, dark and quiet, my cousins, sister-in-law, and I gathered around Nonie's bed. The atmosphere was solemn, and we spoke in hushed tones. Taking hands, we stood around her bed and we all said prayers, lifting Nonie up to heaven and inviting angels to come and escort her to her rest. The Holy Spirit inspired us, the prayer was heartfelt, and we were all moved.

The prayer of the women who loved Nonie was one of the most sacred moments of my life. I was honored to have participated in that act of love. After the prayer was over, I wondered why God was delaying in collecting her. All was ready, why wait? *"Nonie could have come home already but she doesn't want to leave."* This was a surprise to me. Then, *"When a baby is born a woman travails to bring the baby into the world. She does all the work. The birth into eternity is the opposite. The person being born into the next stage makes all the effort. Like an infant birth, the process can be fast, slow, easy, or difficult."*

What a surprise to hear all that! I had no idea my mom was reluctant to leave earth when paradise was waiting for her. She clearly was having a slow and difficult labor. Two days later, Nonie was gone to her reward and it was over. But then a few days later my cousin, Joyous One, had a dream. Nonie had come to her and said "Oh, *you are right Joyous One, it is so beautiful here."* Thank you, Mom, for letting us know you made it safe and sound and that all *was well!*

Later I learned that before I arrived my aunt, Nonie's sister, had visited her. Nonie asked her for forgiveness for something she had carried in her heart and felt remorse over. My aunt assured her that she was forgiven. That was another surprise, my mom having a secret regret. Now I understood why she didn't want to leave. She wasn't sure what her heavenly reception would be. I'm glad she found peace here, and heaven turned out to be beautiful!

After my mom passed away, my dad came to live with my husband and me. He lived with us for thirteen years and during that time we adopted our son, and Dad got to be a grandpa again. As our son Steady Boy grew up, he and Grandpa developed a relationship that was characterized by impatience on both sides. In time, my dad

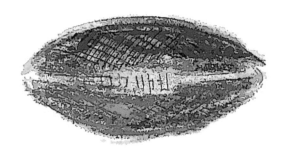

grew infirm and his dance began. After he departed to heaven, again a dream came, this time to his grandson. Steady Boy related:

> *"Last night I had a dream, I was on the beach and Grandpa was with me. He was young like a teenager, and he wanted to throw a ball. So, we ran on the beach and threw a football back and forth to each other and it was fun! Grandpa was really happy!"*

All of this was said with a smile and happy face, no impatience, in remembering Grandpa. I was surprised because I knew that one of my dad's regrets was that he didn't get to have much fun as a child. He was an only son with a very protective mother and disabled father. They didn't want to take any chances and their young child wasn't allowed to play with kids in the neighborhood. The only people safe to play with, according to his parents, were family members so my dad grew up with very few playmates. In kindergarten, he was skipped up to first grade and missed out on the blocks and playtime that he had been looking forward to. At nearly ninety years of age, he still talked about the unfairness of not playing with the blocks like it was yesterday.

The image of the dream was beautiful, and I think it would be perfect if my dad got to play ball with a family member, his grandson, in a dream. Who knows the glories waiting for us in heaven?

I was told that one morning my very ill great-grandmother awoke and said, *"Dette er den beste dagen i mitt liv, for i dag vil jeg se min Kristus."* This translates to *"This is the best day of my life, for today I will see my Christ."* She was right, for that day she went home and met her lord.

> *"Where, O death, is your victory? Where, O death, is your sting?" (1 Corinthians 15:55).*

The gems: We lose our loved ones, we grieve and sit with others in their grief. It is our privilege to do this. We learn that tears flow in the night, but joy comes in the morning. Recognize every day as a special gift and love without hesitation. Appreciate that which is true, noble, right, pure, lovely, admirable, excellent, praiseworthy, and accentuate the positive.

Someday, it will be my turn to dance down the hall to eternity. I hope I have my grandmother's attitude and embrace my birth into heaven with confidence and joy. To be determined . . .

Handbook, Planet Earth

"For this reason I remind you to fan into flame the gift of God, which is in you through the laying on of my hands. For God has not given us a spirit of timidity, but of power, love, and self-control."

2 Timothy 1:6-7

Our Best Defense

This is a most important subject, for we occupy a fallen world, and as the time grows short, the enemy continues to step up his game. We don't usually go around looking for trouble, but when we encounter it, there is a way to fight it. Our best approach is to keep it sweet and simple; the goal is to avoid the snares that are set before us, and when we are caught, to wiggle out. The principles and techniques I have used have been garnered from the wisdom and experience of others. They are tried and true in my experience, and I offer them as solid advice. My main objective is to present true, practical knowledge for the application and retention of freedom.

First principle: Know your enemy. Satan, the father of rebellion, was once the most magnificent of angels but is now a defeated foe and an angry loser. His goal is to destroy as many of God's precious children as possible and take them with him into an eternity separated from the Paradise. He will do this by any means possible. He is called a thief that comes in the night with the goal to kill, steal, and destroy. He is always on the prowl looking for victims.

Second principle: Recognize his presence. The devil and his demons will deceive us and promote trouble any chance they get. They stir up conflict, whisper lies of doubt, bring confusion, and keep us distracted and immobilized. Any time you find yourself in a situation with these elements, raise your antenna and take action. There is an enemy, but it is not your brother, friend, spouse, or any other significant person in your life.

Third principle: Search yourself to see how he got in. We give opportunity when we listen and agree with his deception. Seeds of doubt enter that sprout into vicious weeds. Weeds want to choke out the flowers and dominate the garden but they will only grow as we water and feed them. A weed has a single, sometimes very long and stubborn, root. Plants and flowers have a system of many roots, some big and some small, and are very different in nature. They may look similar at times, but don't be deceived. Once we start on the journey of tending our garden we will recognize the weeds and also recognize them in other people's gardens. They must be removed.

Fourth principle: Extract the root. This is powerful and will change lives. It is a fact that painful and unfair things happen to us. Often, we have no control over these events, but *it's how we react to the unfairness that determines their effect on our lives.* As we become sensitized, we recognize events that have the potential to invite a dark seed. Once the dark seed is in the soil of our heart it will send out a shoot, then grow and take over. The tools for extracting a weed of any size are these:

Go before the cross. Verbally confess what we did that hurt ourselves and/or another person as a result of our reaction to the event. Give it all to God, lay it at the foot of the cross, and give up the burden. There is nothing we can ever do to make things right, even the score, or take back our power. It is a futile effort and not our battle to fight.

Take authority. After the confession declare that in the name of Jesus this child is forgiven and free, and these sins are buried in the sea of God's forgetfulness. Whom the Son sets free is free indeed! It is important to remember that soon the devil will come back and tell us that nothing happened with that prayer, etc., so expect it. He wants to make us doubt and question.

Always assume there is a spiritual component. Verbally say *"In the name and the power and the authority of Jesus Christ of Nazareth, we rebuke you Satan, and any spirit that does not bow down to the name of Jesus. You must release and depart from this child of God because he/she is forgiven and you have no foothold here anymore. You must go where Jesus tells you to go. Be gone in the name of Jesus of Nazareth."* Any combination of these words is good, they all work. We say *Jesus of Nazareth* because that's what he told his disciples to say when instructing them in using his name for healing. The name of Jesus of Nazareth clearly defines whose name we are using to give us authority to cast the dark side out.

Speak scripture as the final word to seal the deal. One that is easy to remember is *I belong to God, and greater is He in me than you who are in the world and you must go.* The word of God defeats the devil and Jesus gave us that example when he was tempted by Satan in the wilderness. The spoken word of God is a weapon suitable for the pulling down of strongholds and fortresses in heavenly places!

Fifth principle: Say thank you and walk away in freedom. When you are approached again by the devil, and he suggests something which is a lie, just say out loud, *"I'm not signing that contract and I rebuke you in the name, the power and the authority of Jesus Christ of Nazareth, you are under my feet."* This can all be said in a whisper if needed, he hears it loud and clear.

Recognize the sin, confess the sin, ask forgiveness for the sin, declare forgiveness for the sin, rebuke and cast down the devil in the name of Jesus Christ of Nazareth, speak a scripture and he will flee, thank God and walk away restored to wholeness. Simple and it can all be done in a few minutes. *"For You, Lord, are good, and ready to forgive, and abundant in loving kindness to all who call upon You" (Psalm 86:5).*

The gems: There are many mistakes we can make in life and the enemy is vigilant. God is always there, ready to set us free. Ultimately, our sins will be separated from us as far as the east is from the west as long as we give them to him.

We can't mess it up because the result doesn't depend on us, only on God! Keep it simple and sweet, it is our best defense!

75

Doors of Opportunity

Doors are wonderful things to knock on, open, and walk through. They come in all shapes, styles, and sizes, something for everyone. Often, we have been invited and occasionally we invite ourselves. We all hear gentle tapping at the doors of our hearts, sometimes it's a tap of invitation and sometimes it's a tap of temptation. Sometimes it's a chorus of taps, and we have to decide between door number 1, door number 2, or door number 3. Doors are opportunity, just push through and see what's on the other side! One door closes, another door opens.

When I was a teenager, I became curious about supernatural things after someone gave me a Ouija board. It seemed strange but my girlfriends and I played with great excitement, usually at night with the lights low, accompanied by heart-pounding questions and squeals of laughter. As usual my mom wanted to rain on my parade with scripture. She really knew how to ruin a good party. So there she was reminding me of God's opinion on the subject, but come on now, that was for people who lived thousands of years ago. Right?

> *"There shall not be found among you anyone who makes his son or his daughter pass through the fire, one who uses divination, one who practices witchcraft, or one who interprets omens, or a sorcerer, or one who casts a spell, or a medium, or a spiritist,*

or one who calls up the dead. For whoever does these things is detestable to the LORD; and because of these detestable things the LORD your God will drive them out before you" (Deuteronomy 18:11).

After a while, I became uncomfortable with some of the messages the Ouija board spelled out, so I decided to stop playing with it. However, even though I had tossed it out and moved on with no damage done, or so I thought, something had changed. My peace was gone.

Usually at night, my head would hit the pillow, and I was in snooze land. Now I started hearing footsteps in the hall and in my room at night. I felt a presence that frightened me. Even my younger brother heard the footsteps! I would lie in bed and pray for God to make the "activity" stop so I could go to sleep. This went on intermittently for the next few years while I lived in my parents' home. When I was in my late teens, I moved to the city to attend school. I thought by moving I would leave the nonsense behind. But no, I still had odd occurrences in my apartment. My radio had a habit of turning itself off and on. Then my mom learned about familiar spirits and told me about them. She prayed over me, rebuked them in Jesus's name, and she taught me how to send demons back where they came from. A new and very useful lesson. Yet, as I continued on my life journey, paranormal activity continued here and there, and I became somewhat used to it. Just one of those things.

Fast-forward a dozen years. I am earnestly seeking, enjoying Christian growth, transforming, and house cleaning. I loved to read and often visited the local Christian bookstore. Learning was wonderful! One day I picked up a book about Christians who unwittingly harbor dark spirits even though they have the Lord in their lives. Apparently the two entities can coexist in a person.

Fascinated, I started reading this book. It contained a wealth of information that was never discussed in church. As I read this book, I saw myself. I have learned time and again that God directs the lessons in my life. He presents the next big thing on his agenda for my growth and freedom. So here it was, the next thing on his plan for me; and the more I read, the more I knew I needed freedom.

As I read the book, I recognized some of the symptoms described by the authors. I knew that demons of the dark side were real, and I was eager to find out what this meant for me. My mother had prayed over me, and I believed myself totally forgiven and free. However, I still experienced occurrences of nonsense and here was new information.

At the time I was part of a small prayer and share home group. We met in my home weekly and the number of attendees varied from four to twelve. There was a small structured time of praise and a lesson, then we shared what was going in in our lives and prayed for each other. I knew I had to approach this subject, but how should I do it? That week only four people attended the meeting, including myself. Two were new believers, but we were all close, and I knew it would be all right. When we came to the sharing part of the evening, I didn't know what to say but launched out anyway. As  I started talking about the book and its message, it suddenly was clear to me what I needed to do. I would never have thought of this, but the Holy Spirit led me in his marvelous way. I had invited the enemy of God into my life by opening the door and playing with the Ouija board. I hadn't thought of this in years and was as surprised as everyone else to hear myself say it. So now what? Not knowing exactly what would happen I had the two new believers sit on the other side of the table and my wonderful co-leader, Gentle Friend, picked up The Sword of the word.

One of the points in the book is that when a spirit makes its exit, something is expelled from the body. Laughter, yawning, vomiting, hiccups, burping, tears were all candidates. It is also good to open a window and invite the spirit to vacate the premises. I prayed and poured out my heart to the Lord as we do in such moments. I asked for forgiveness for dabbling in that which was forbidden and disobeying God's instructions. And as I prayed, the oddest thing began to happen. Tears with the intensity of a geyser began spurting from my eyes. Tears that didn't have anything to do with the ordinary kind of tears that well up in the eyes and roll down the cheeks. I confessed my sin, asked for forgiveness, Gentle Friend prayed over me to be healed, he rebuked the enemy and told him to leave, and declared me free in Jesus's name. And I was free!

I knew something important had happened, and I was free from a tower of imprisonment. In the days that followed, I was aware that a static, or interference, previously present, was gone. Now my perception was different, crystal clear, and peaceful. That confession was one of  the best moves I ever made. I would never have known if the Holy Spirit, who leads us into all knowledge of the truth, had not revealed it to me. My mom's initial efforts were a good first step but the root of disobedience goes deep. Her praying over me, without my owning the actions and asking for forgiveness, did not set me free.

The first commandment says it all, "*You shall have no other gods before me*" *(Exodus 20:3)*. We can minimize and dismiss things we have done in darkness, but that doesn't mean the attachment has been broken. Some things I learned were: Once I allow rebellion into my life the dark side is given a foothold and will occupy until forcibly removed; if God says something is forbidden, believe it; if I weaken and eat the apple anyway, make amends as soon as possible; align my thoughts and actions with what I believe is the heart of God and let his agenda be my agenda.

God takes very seriously the opening of a door that leads to consulting with the father of lies. Fortunately, his word gives us the action to take: *"So they went out and preached that the people should repent. They also drove out many demons and healed many of the sick, anointing them with oil." (Mark 6:12–13)*

I have come to think of dark spirits that attach to us through deception, like helium balloons. They are tied to our wrist, float nearby, and follow us like a constant companion. When we confess and they are rebuked, the string is cut and off they float into the wild blue yonder. Bye, bye! God set boundaries for navigating planet earth, first for his glory and second for our well-being.

> *"Those I love, I rebuke and discipline. Therefore, be earnest and repent. Behold, I stand at the door and knock. If anyone hears My voice and opens the door, I will come in and dine with him, and he with Me. To the one who is victorious, I will grant the right to sit with Me on My throne, just as I overcame and sat down with My Father on His throne." (Revelation 3:20)*

> *"You, Lord, are forgiving and good, abounding in love to all who call on you." (Psalm 86:5)*

The gems: A knock of temptation will offer a false reward. Once the door is opened our territory is invaded. We live accommodating the enemy in our lives. We can take action to route the enemy, then keep our kingdom green, lush and protected. Our God is forgiving and his word says, *"Above all else guard your heart, for everything you do flows from it." (Proverbs 4:23)*

The door that connects our natural realm, with the unseen spiritual realm, has only one knob, and it is on our side. There is only one person who determines the action to take in response to the knocking. Find out who is on the other side of the door first. Be cautious. Living free and clear is awesome, and I recommend it to anyone!

Inner Vows and the Little Princess

Back in the vast and dimly meanwhile of my childhood, I became a big sister. This did not line up with my agenda. I was the princess and my crown was not coming off . . . until it did. This is a story that I share because it was a great lesson and princess-itis can affect anyone.

I was born a most wanted child, adored by parents and grandparents. I was strong-willed and did my best to make sure everyone knew my scepter and tiara, even though plastic, were *real*. My world was perfect, filled with love, affection, pretty dresses, sleepovers with my grandparents, playdates with my cousin and neighborhood friends to boss around. I was living the life! But at age four, our family moved from a rented house to a new one my parents designed and built themselves. I had my own room now! That day, my tidy gene switched on, and it has been humming ever since. Furniture arranged just so, shoes lined up in the closet, all objects on the dresser intentionally placed. My mom got lovely prints of the masterpieces Pinkie and the Blue Boy, that I requested, for the walls. Their elegance had just the right touch and my world went from great to amazing!

One day our neighbor said very casually to me, "How nice your mom is having a baby." *What? No, she is NOT having a baby!* That was my first clue, but I dismissed it as incomprehensible. Now, I had noticed that my mom seemed to have a beach ball under her blouse but that never struck me as something to even wonder about. She was mom and if she had grown two heads it wouldn't have mattered.

Then one night I was woken up, driven to my grandparents' house, left there, and I had no idea what was going on. No one said a word to me. I just sat there and waited for them to come back. After a couple of days, I finally saw the family car coming down the road, and I was so excited! Until it drove right by me without even slowing down.

My grandparents put me in their car and off we went. I was finally going home. When we arrived, we were met by a woman I had never seen before in my life. I didn't care, I only wanted my mommy! I ran down the hall, saw her in bed, and immediately jumped on her so glad to have her back. But the woman's strong arms pulled me away, and I was told she was too weak and I had to stand back. Then, to my right I saw it. A crib complete with a sleeping baby in it. I took all this in and knew I could not change it. I turned around, marched out to the car where my grandfather was waiting, got in, and said, *"Let's go home, Grandpa."* And that was the beginning of my inner vow, *"I will never love or accept my brother."*

We all make inner vows as we go through life. They are mechanisms we employ to safeguard our hearts. Inner vows protect us but also prevent our growth. There is no stepping out in courage to accept new challenges, lessons, and blessings. Everything stops right there.

The years went by and my little brother was merely a nuisance to me. Not a friend, an ally or important in any way. It never even crossed my mind that it should be any different. Very sad to look back on later. My little brother, Steady and True, never knew why his sister was so distant. Never knew a big sister was someone who was supposed to be on your side. We were just two kids living under the same roof, dealing with the same parents. I turned nineteen, moved out, started college, and as usual, never looked back. For a few years anyway, then I got a new perspective.

Now that my brother and I were adults, a new relationship was forged. We had things in common, and I enjoyed seeing him at family occasions. Steady and True had chosen to go to Bible college and followed the path of Jesus. I followed the path of the world and kept my faith to myself. It wasn't a secret, just private.

Steady and True met a lovely woman, got married, and started a family. I moved and found a church I could plug into and find fellowship, at last. Now it was time to take a look at myself, and did I ever! God loves us as we are, but he loves us too much to let us stay that way. The Holy Spirit was working overtime in cleaning out the horded rooms and dark closets of my heart, and I couldn't have been happier!

Friday night and back to the bookstore for a new supply of reading material. I found just the ticket for a new work in my life about inner vows. I read about them and was energized! I imagined so many of my friends carrying heavy bags of emotional weight and was totally compassionate in my desire to ease their burdens. I couldn't imagine bearing the weight of family dramas, how awful, how unnecessary! I was so glad I had a family that got along and supported each other. Why, I had the perfect family, and I was the perfect vessel for God to bring the message of breaking inner vows to my friends! How clever God was to choose me! And then I heard the words, *"What about your brother?"*

Huh? My brother? That was so long ago, and nobody cares now do they? Well, maybe they didn't care now, but it seemed God still did. He would not let me rest until I had a plan. So, in my desire to bring healing to my friends, it seemed I was the first candidate for the process. That weekend I drove an hour to my parents' home. It was evening, dinner was served, very nice, but that was not the main course for me. No, I had something different on the menu for that evening. *How can you say to your brother, let me take the speck out of your eye, while there is still a beam in your own eye? You hypocrite! First take the beam out of your own eye, and then you will see clearly to remove the speck from your brother's eye (Matthew 7:4-5).* I believe God has a sense of humor and gets a good laugh out of some of our pompous nonsense!

After the plates had been cleared away, I opened with the statement, *"I've been thinking about when Steady and True was born and my reaction to it."* Not exactly what my parents were expecting to hear, but I had never been an easy child. Dead silence, and then we had an engaging and honest conversation about that fateful event. I asked their forgiveness for being a princess and thinking everything was only about me.

My dad paced around, tears glinting in his eyes. *I knew we didn't do the right thing, not telling you. We just didn't know how.* My mom was bewildered and didn't know what to say at first. Then, *Steady never knew why you were so distant from him. His life was missing the love of a big sister.* I telephoned my brother and asked for his forgiveness. Of course, without a second thought, he said he forgave me. And I knew that he had been forgiving me for many years. Thank you, dear brother! What an unexpected outcome from reading a book that shared a concept I had never heard of before. To me it was a miracle, certainly not an everyday occurrence. To this day, I am grateful for the inspiration and the courage to acknowledge my error and act to rectify my actions. Only the Holy Spirit could have put that together!

So, what was the lesson in this? Well, for starters, nothing really gets buried and forgotten. I think we adapt and do the best we can with situations, but they never completely vanish. The only way to really be free is to acknowledge its presence, haul it up, and expose it to the light of day. Examine it, repent and ask for forgiveness as appropriate. Then hold it in open hands and release it to heaven. Let it fly away and be truly gone. I thought about why I needed to go through this exercise. It was all in the past, our family was happy and loving toward each other. *So why now?* I believe that I was obedient to the leading of the Holy Spirit. And as usual, it wasn't only about me. My parents had carried guilt with them for years. My brother had been puzzled, and I had been self-centered for years. Humbling myself to my family brought about a healing that could never have taken place with my silence. *"My sacrifice, O God, is a broken spirit; a broken and contrite heart you, God, will not despise" (Psalm 51:17).*

The gems: Self-centeredness can hurt ourselves and others. I was released from my selfishness; my parents were released from their silence and my brother was released from wondering what he did wrong. Not knowing the limited number of years I would have with my brother, I am grateful. Who the son sets free, is free indeed. Forgiveness is a gift from heaven! In the end, it is all about God, how he whispers to us, and directs our steps. Our best move is just to follow him and stay on his path.

Now, Who Did I Say I Am?

This is a loaded question: *Who am I?* I have asked myself this question many times and never had a good answer. I will say that in retrospect I have had many chapters in my life, and they have all added up to "who I am now." And the "who I am now" may only be temporary. Each period of my life, depending on where I lived, schools, friends, professions,  hobbies, relationships, etc., was a new dimension and evolution of my persona. One thing leads to another. In casting my thoughts back in time, to ponder my psychological roots, I discovered an unlikely friend and ally. My ever-present shell collection!

Let me tell you about my shell collection. When I was very small, my parents would take me to the beach to play, and I would look for shells. I loved to chase the seagulls, collect the shells in my bucket, and bring them home. Later, when I was in fourth grade, my teacher divided our class into two groups. We had to choose between being a rock hound or a shell collector. I debated between the two as I loved both sparkly minerals and smooth, interesting shells. The shells won as I preferred the idea of walking on the beach looking for shells rather than walking in the dirt looking for rocks. Our teacher handed out the pieces of our collections and taught us about each one them. I had a flat box that I kept my shells in, each labeled and ready for the next lesson. And when fourth grade was over, there was my shell collection. What should I do with it? Not having the heart to throw it away and not having anyone to give it to, the box went into my closet.

If the shells could talk, they would have a lot to say about how my life evolved. The shells would tell you that, as an elementary school student, I was ridiculed and mocked by older girls. I didn't even know them, but they would come to my classroom window, make faces at me, stick out their tongues, call me names, and then run away. Maybe it was because I had discovered Barbie dolls and preferred to dress in coordinated outfits with matching shoes?

My shells could tell you about the day I walked to the local park to play on the swings. As I walked through the parking lot, I saw a group of girls standing at the edge where the gravel started. I approached them to head for the swings on the other side, and one of them stepped toward me. *"Go home, we don't want you here."* Never in my life had I encountered that kind of behavior. I just stood there, not sure what to do. Then the girls, maybe ten to twelve of them and a little older than me, picked up stones and threw them at me! I wasn't hurt, but I turned around and went home. This was my first experience that the world could be a dangerous, and hateful, place.

In junior high, my shells saw I was even more of an outcast. My family had moved to a new town, and I had a new school with no friends. I also was shy, so the label I heard most often was "Stuck-Up." I could not bear to wear my glasses anymore due to *Seventeen Magazine* standards, and walked around blind, bumping into things. Often, I went to the nurse's office with a stomachache and my mom would come and get me, take me to the doctor's office, and he could never find anything wrong with me. At that point I didn't know

about rejection-itis, but that was the problem. I was in a new school with hundreds of kids I didn't know, had acne, a challenging mom, a brother I couldn't relate to, and a brainiac dad who couldn't believe I hadn't inherited one single practical or mathematical gene. Eventually, I made friends, got contact lenses, and felt connected but I could never shake Stuck-Up.

At age nineteen, I got a job and was headed for the big city and a new life. I packed my things and there on the pile, out from the closet, was my box of shells. Somehow it felt right that they should go with me, so into the car they went. After that, over the years, each time I moved the shells went with me to take up residence in a new closet. Years later, I was introduced to the brandy snifter as the perfect display case for shells! I bought one, arranged my shells in it, and threw away the box! At last my shells were out of the closet! I added to my collection and also bought a shell night-light that still burns brightly in my life.

I have been a doggie mama and a cat lady most of my life with only brief exceptions. Having a sweet fur baby, or two or three, was part of my life. Animals go a long way in filling the voids in our lives. Many of my friends had walked down the aisle of wedded bliss, and I was still single. One day I checked out the personal ads in the newspaper. Hmmm, everyone seemed to be brilliant, multifaceted, talented, climbed Mount Everest on the weekend, and had important careers. Well, that left me out. At the time I had recently lost my two cats and dog to old-age-syndrome and was now pet-free. This made for an empty apartment, but I was free from responsibility and enjoying it. Until one day, my co-worker brought a puppy to work  to give away. "NO," I said! But by the end of the day, I had weakened and brought the little black, curly bundle into my office just to visit for a moment. Ha! That was the end for me! By five o'clock, I had a new dog and was so *happy*! I was in love! Trina was the dog I gave birth to, and she was the perfect blessing for me at that time. When

I met my husband many years later, he asked me to choose between him and my dog. Well that was a no-brainer! Eventually he learned to share and we all got along!

The shells continued to watch from their glass house as I shared my life with my little black dog, hosted share groups, birthday parties, and celebrated holidays with my friends. Life was good, but my shells saw me still searching . . . looking for love, a meaningful life purpose, and my true identity. Then, one day, I decided to consult God on the subject.

Who am I God? Amazing how fast he answers when it is the right question. *"You are a citizen of heaven and a sojourner on Earth."* That was it, a short answer but a new truth for me. I could not have been more surprised! I pondered his answer that my name is written in the Lamb's Book of Life; therefore, I am a future resident of heaven. For now, I journeyed on the path God had for my earthly life.

God's truth is always simple! I thought about all the adjectives that could be used to describe a person. They all involved positive attributes, accomplishments, wit, charm, beauty, talent, and temporary positions in life. The reality is we all have jobs, friends, spouses, and children that come and go. I may not always be a doggie mama. Someday I will be retired. So how do I define my eternal-self by these temporary stages of life? That is where God's big picture comes in. My temporary earth-journey now is to prepare me to be an eternal citizen of heaven later. Not a maybe, or an if, but a certainty.

Knowing this truth really helped me when I felt insecure. Like when I made the decision to exit the industry I had been involved in for many years. Wanting something different for my life, I went back to school to learn new

things and have new opportunities. Breaking free felt great but now I was sitting in classes with kids much younger than me. So now who was I? That was a good question since many of my friends had moved away and moved on in life. I was no longer involved with the Bible study that had filled my life for so long. It had run its course and now it was time to grow and stretch on our own. With regret to leave the former behind, and an uncertain future, all I could do was step out and be brave. A new job in a new field, full time school, computers, and homework. But I made the adjustment and went through the no-man's-land of shifting sand because I really did know who I was! I had no accolades, no new degree, position, or title. But I knew who I was, I knew with certainty that I was a citizen of heaven. The more I pondered it, the better it got. I had peace in my heart even though the world was not impressed with me. I knew that God loved me, he had died for me, and I was on a good path and on solid ground. *"But our citizenship is in heaven. And we eagerly await a Savior from there, the Lord Jesus Christ." (Philippians 3:20)*

By this time my parents had moved to another state, so I didn't even have them to visit. But no self-pity for me. This was the time when I finally felt comfortable in my own skin. I had gained spiritual self-confidence and been released from the world system that had defined me. I learned to not judge myself, relax, and walk according to the truth and lessons of the moment. The Bible says his word is like a two-edged sword that pierces both the one who gives it, and the one who receives it. Recently I received a beautiful visual from the Lord along the same principle. As soldiers in battle, we are given weapons and equipment. One of these weapons is the shield of faith. I looked up and saw a shield lifted high, gleaming and lightweight. Easy to raise to deflect the stones and arrows that come our way. On the inside of the shield I saw the words "God loves me." On the outside of the shield, I saw the words "God loves you." A shield that gives protection in the fray, and the promise of hope to all. A win-win shield!

"Stand firm then, with the belt of truth fastened around your waist, with the breastplate of righteousness arrayed, and with your feet fitted with the readiness of the gospel of peace. In addition to all this, take up the shield of faith, with which you can extinguish all the flaming arrows of the evil one."
(Ephesians 6:14–16)

My lovely shell collection of peace and beauty appeared in my life seemingly by chance many years ago, but I know it was for God's purpose. Today, I keep my shells on display in their brandy snifter and move them around occasionally so they can enjoy different rooms. Over time I have added many lovely gifts of shells from family and friends.

The gems: We come into this world a blank slate. We discover who we are and make the best of it. When Jesus comes into our hearts, our names are recorded in the Lamb's Book of Life and we become citizens of heaven. We write a new story on our slate, we journey with a new purpose, we receive unexpected gifts of love, we see ourselves and others with new eyes, and we find out exactly who we really are! And sometimes we not only get rocks, we also get shells!

I look forward to the next leg of my journey as a citizen in heaven and would love to find my shells have been magically beamed up and are there waiting for me!

Musings, Ponderings and Adventures of the Heart

"When I consider Your heavens, the work of your fingers,
The moon and the stars, which you have set in place,
what is mankind that you are mindful of them,
human beings that you care for them?"

Psalm 8:3–4

Are Names Important?

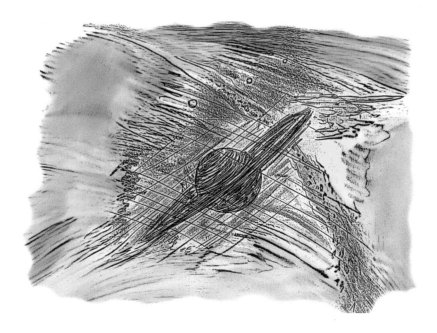

How important is a name? A name is personal, it gives us our identity and tells other people who we are. God named Adam, Adam named the animals, and then Eve came along. We have had husbands, wives, cows, dogs, pigs, and gazelles ever since. And it is very embarrassing if we call someone by the wrong name!

Throughout the Bible are genealogies of people with unpronounceable names who don't seem important to the story line but they're in there anyway. Apparently it seems to God that people and names matter.

God himself has many names that mean different things and here are just a few.

- ELOHIM: God "Creator, Mighty and Strong"
- YAHWEH-SHALOM: "The Lord Our Peace"
- YAHWEH-ROHI: "The Lord Our Shepherd"

- EL ELYON: "Most High"
- EL-OLAM: "Everlasting God"

When we were born, our parents gave us names that were meaningful to them. How exciting to know that in our next phase we will get names from God himself, our eternal parent. They will be so meaningful and private that no one will know them but us! Jesus will have his name *King of Kings and Lord of Lords* displayed on his robe and body as he charges into Armageddon on a white warhorse! The Name of Jesus will win the war, and he will get his own private name from the Father, too!

> *"On his robe and on his thigh, he has this name written: king of kings and lord of lords." (Revelation 19:16)*

> *"His eyes are like blazing fire, and on his head, are many crowns. He has a name written on him that no one knows but he himself." (Revelation 19:12)*

"Whoever has ears, let them hear what the Spirit says to the churches. To the one who is victorious, I will give some of the hidden manna. I will also give that person a white stone with a new name written on it, known only to the one who receives it." (Revelation 2:17)

We didn't have a name picked out for our child, and it was only days away from show time. I had painted the nursery pink, so sure I was that our birth mom carried a girl. Then suddenly, out of the blue, I knew our birth mom carried a boy, and he would have brown eyes and reddish-brown hair. I knew the name I wanted was that of my brother who had departed for heaven in the prime of his life. It made me happy to think that his name would live on in our home. And I knew it would honor my brother's memory and that is exactly what happened.

What about the little lives that never get their first glimpse of this world? Some named and grieved over, some disposed of and forgotten. Do they have a special place in God's realm? And the children that die before the age of accountability? Yes, of course they do, they go straight into his presence! *"Blessed are the pure in heart: for they shall see God." (Matthew 5:8)*

When we have a special project, we call it "our baby." We love our babies and will move mountains to protect and nurture them. I think Jesus had a baby, too, and her name was Jerusalem. He watched over her, and her walls were ever before him. His city, his love, the one he cried over. In the end, he will redeem

her and bring her forth, a holy city, a new Jerusalem. She will be his treasure forever, his domain of peace, beauty and joy.

> *"Can a mother forget the baby at her breast*
> *and have no compassion on the child she has borne?*
> *Though she may forget, I will not forget you! See, I*
> *have engraved you on the palms of my hands; your*
> *walls are ever before me." (Isaiah 49: 15-16)*

The name of Jesus means *God saves*, and I believe that all human life is precious to him, no matter how small it is when it departs. He takes all the little lives and loves them in his heavenly domain. Jesus is the one who loves little children!

For those who grieve or have regrets, I believe there will be a joy-filled reunion to look forward to in a place where all our tears are dried.

When my husband and I were on our quest to find a birth mom, we met a few candidates. Twice we thought we had found the one for us but were disappointed. They each found that pregnancy was too inconvenient and ended our hopes. I believe that someday I will meet the little lives that we wanted to hold and love here on this earth. For the present time they are in good hands!

So, let us celebrate the name above all names! Jesus, our living water and our rock!

"Salvation is found in no one else, for there is no other name under heaven given to mankind by which we must be saved." (Acts 4:12)

Yes, names are important for he knows each one of us by name and someday we will get new, very special ones!

Gabriel's Mission

The following story had its beginning in a morning church service I attended. The congregation was singing and praising God, worshipping with arms outstretched and the music was glorious. Then, high overhead, up near the ceiling, I saw motion.

A flutter. Angel's wings?

Once I have seen something, I can't look away, so I set my mind free to follow the wings and see where they would lead. And lead they did! Straight up into heaven where an important meeting was taking place. There in the Sacred Council Chamber the Father and Son were in deep discussion.

"The time has come to launch our plan. The regime is in place that will carry our message to the farthest corners of the world and there is written language to record the events. The Roman cross that will forever distinguish you has been established and my people are awaiting their Messiah." The planning took shape and any general knows that troops are best equipped when accompanied by a buddy, someone who has their back.

"Two are better than one because they have a good return for their labor. For if either of them falls, the one will lift up his companion. But woe to

the one who falls when there is not another to lift him up." (Ecclesiastes 4:9–10)

The Father summoned one of his highest-ranking angels, namely me, to join the meeting. *Gabriel, I am bestowing on you the honor of protecting my son as he goes forth to engage the world and win it back for our purpose and glory. Everything is held in the balance of his success and he must not fail.*

You will be near him at all times should he need strengthening or encouragement. Your job is to oversee all the elements of our plan and ensure its success.

So that's how it started. The battle gear wasn't exactly what I would have expected for such a mission. In place of an array of weapons was a single, mighty sword. In place of a war room was a stable and a carpenter's workshop. In place of well-trained troops, there were twelve men and a few women.

Yes, sir, at your service. We will not fail!

Thank you, Gabriel. Your first assignment is to go and meet a certain young handmaiden named Mary. She has been chosen for the highest honor among all women, and you will invite her to join our mission.

I dispatched forthwith to deliver the message I had been charged with. Mary was both surprised and composed. She did a lot better than most people do upon seeing an angel and receiving instructions. But then again, she had been born for this day and her words were beautiful. *"I am the Lord's servant, Mary answered. May your word to me be fulfilled. Then the angel left her." (Luke 1:38)*

Now the team was complete and the Father hung a glorious star in the heavens to herald the approach of the coming king. In the east lived Magi, men of wisdom and magic, who studied the stars. They

saw the brilliant sphere and understood its significance. The wise men set out on a journey with precious gifts to honor the one the star proclaimed.

As the time grew near for the birth of the king, I escorted Mary and Joseph on the long trek to Bethlehem. Not an easy journey for someone in Mary's condition. Then I hovered over the stable and at the first cry of the babe I joined the angels assembled over the fields to proclaim the news, "Hallelujah, glory in the highest!"

The men from the east arrived at the stable and presented their gifts to the one they found there. No questions asked, it didn't

matter the circumstances of the nursery. They knew what they knew and their timing was perfect. A day sooner the baby would not have been born yet, a few days later he would have been gone. They followed their hearts and marveled at the glory of God. They laid their gifts before the babe and rejoiced that they had beheld the King of Kings! To this day wise men still seek him, and that tiny stable is the most famous one in the world!

The sacred babe was presented in the temple and named Jesus as instructed, which means "God saves his people."

As the years passed, I was always close at hand. One time the child's parents mistakenly left him behind in the city, then came racing back in panic. Not the first parents to do that, but they need not have worried. I was on the job.

More children were born to Mary and Joseph, and it was a busy household. Jesus was an attentive big brother, and even with sibling rivalry, they were a close family. It was understood that the firstborn son had a special calling, and they all supported that, even if they didn't understand what it was. In due time, Jesus learned his father's trade, as did his brothers, but his work would not be there for long.

Then, in what seemed like no time at all, it was time to go see his cousin, John the Baptist, at the Jordan river. Jesus was baptized, and I had a little "angel to man" talk with him about the next phase of his mission.

"It's time to get the show on the road and do not get distracted by any women! Concentrate on the men you will call to be your followers and fulfill the prophesies made to your people. They have waited a long time, this is IT and there is no turning back!"

Those were amazing years for the mission. Lepers were healed, the blind saw, the lame leaped, the demonized were set free, and the dead lived again. Truth was dispensed and people believed. Food was multiplied and there were lessons on walking on water. Of course, there was some dissension in the ranks but most of the time the team was on task. Except for one . . . It seemed he wanted to earn a little extra money on the side.

Three short years later, it was time to prepare his followers for the coming days. The last night celebrating the Passover was a night to

remember. Washing of feet and establishing the communion of believers, Jesus was an example of strength and humility, and I was proud of him. Later the going got tough, but he did not back down. I hoped my words of encouragement had helped and even now he could look to me any time he felt weak. Jesus had been my responsibility and we were both in it to win it! The last night and day were the hardest and no mortal man could have done it. One may think that angels don't have emotions but that is not true. We cry, too.

I thought about the preparations that had been made in heaven and knew all was ready. In front of the mighty throne of the Father stood a table made of gold. On the table was an urn made of solid gold and inlaid with sparkling jewels, waiting. Now the first blows were heard as the nails were driven into the cross on the hill. I knew the blows reverberated throughout paradise. The heavenly host was somber and sad as they watched heaven's hope go through the final test.

Ministering angels had been assigned the duty of collecting the sacred blood of the lamb. Throughout the day, they flew from heaven to Calvary, and back again. Each drop of the divinely human blood was collected and deposited in the golden urn before the Father's throne. This event would always be known as the Sacred Pilgrimage of Atonement, and the attending angels could not have asked for a higher honor.

The shape of the urn echoed the chalice shared by Jesus and his followers on the previous evening. A ceremony that would be remembered and continued by the faithful. As the blood was deposited in the urn, sparks of color  flashed from its jewels, marking the progress of the sacrifice. Once every drop of blood was in the urn, the next phase of the mission would begin. The urn didn't have long to wait, events were moving along according to plan.

Along with legions of angels, I hovered above the hill waiting. The divinely human man below was suffering and paying the wages of mans' sin, according to the plan. It was almost complete. I could see Mary, with her children and the followers of Jesus, below. They waited for the end, and with it their dreams, their faith and their belief in Messiah crushed. Drawing forward toward the cross then falling back, tears flowing, devastated. If it had been permitted, I would have offered them the comfort of a

word that this scene was all part of the plan. Then the voice cried out, "Father, into your hands I commit my spirit."

Sacrificial death for the sake of mankind, check! This was the moment I was waiting for, and down I went like a flash of lightening to receive the divine spirit as it was released from the mortal, beaten, bloodied, body. Hallelujah!

Free and clear, not a moment to lose! Two angels came forward to oversee the lowering of the body from the cross and be stationed in the tomb. The angels watching above wanted to celebrate and cheer, but there would be time for that later. Now the angels took position and launched out, speeding south for the next target. I fell in beside Jesus, followed by the attending angels through the atmosphere, to the next stage of the mission: free the hostages.

In record time, we were there, in front of the mighty gates of hell. Jesus alone touched down in front of the gates in close proximity to the heat. No opposition greeted him, just the silence of doom. Jesus extended his arms and opened his hand to reveal the object he held: the keys of hell. There was a new sheriff in town, and it was time to clean house.

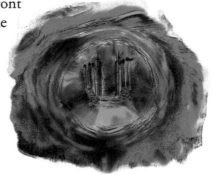

The gates swung open and in he went, victorious, strong, and purposeful. I did not follow Jesus but floated in the sky over the fiery gates. A host of angels formed a canopy of holiness at the edge of evil.

Black and White, never the twain shall meet. Our job was to wait.

This was the moment that Jesus had looked forward to for ages, and I could well imagine what was happening below. I could see Jesus descending and entering the bosom of Abraham, or Hades, where the faithful awaited their messiah. He had one message to give and would not waste a moment. Each man and woman in that dark place would get the chance to look into the eyes of Jesus and hear the words:

"I am the way and the truth and the life. No one comes to the Father except through me. Today is the Day of Atonement and I am the Lamb of God. Will you receive the sacrifice of my blood shed for you and have eternal life in paradise with me?"

Did anyone say "No thanks"? Not likely. Then the gates swung open and out came the Victorious One followed by the ransomed ones. As they emerged the angels dived in to form a hedge of protection, a heavenly escort. As they jetted out, I fell in last to protect the most amazing rescue effort ever conducted on the behalf of humans. Scores of souls trapped behind enemy lines and now *all set free!*

He is mighty to save! Well, after all, we are heaven's special forces. Redeem the captives, check! The heavenly contingent sped through the vast expanse north and then ahead were the lights of heaven glistening and welcoming. Darkness into light! How beautiful and wonderful it was, there are no words to describe this one and only chartered flight to freedom!

Heaven glowed with golden radiance as the angels swooped in with their charges, delivered safe and sound. Jesus and I nodded to the angels on duty at the gate, turned, and headed south. The empty tomb was waiting.

When we arrived at the tomb the angels, left to preside over the burial, were standing by eager to proceed. When a spirit leaves a body the heart stops beating, breathing ceases, the spirit slips from the body and the silver cord is broken. Now it was the opposite. The

spirit reentered the body with a surge of energy, like a strong electric shock administered to restart a heart. Energy entered and filled every cell with a blinding flash that seared the image of the beaten body onto the shroud that covered it. The silver cord shot through, reattached, and the spirit was back! The unrecognizable body of the man laid to rest was gone. In his place rose a man glorious with health and wholeness. I signaled to the attending angels to roll the stone away.

Resurrection accomplished, check!

Outside the tomb, the sun was rising and footsteps approached. A woman peered into the empty tomb brushing tears from her eyes.

Woman, why are you weeping? Who are you looking for? Sir, if you have carried Him off, tell me where you have put Him, and I will get Him. Mary. And turning around, *Rabboni!*

Then Mary knew it was Jesus and her sadness turned to joy! She wanted to reach out and cling to the miracle before her but was told *no.* Jesus had not presented himself to the father yet so the reunion would have to wait. Instead Mary was instructed to return to the brothers and tell them the good news.

I signaled to Jesus that it was time to go then we were flying north through the heavens to the next step of the mission. We arrived and gates of pearl opened before us. Beyond was a welcoming party like no other! Myriads of angels filled the arena as the

Victorious One made his way to his Father's throne.

"This is my son, whom I love; with him I am well pleased!" Hosannas rang out and cheers of joy poured forth from the heavenly

host and the ransomed ones!!! The pardoned thief on the cross wept for joy to see his Savior!

Jesus strode with confidence to the golden table and looked into his Father's eyes. He lifted the bejeweled lid and placed it on the Golden Urn which was now filled with his own living ruby-red blood. Holding it high for all to see, the words rang out, *"It is finished!"* Then Jesus turned and entered the inner sanctum that held the Arc of the Covenant and the Mercy Seat. Jesus placed the urn on the center of the Mercy Seat, the final act of the redemption. Jesus was now the people's High  Priest in the order of Melchizedek! In this new role his greatest joy would be to cover the sins of anyone who came to him in faith. All were welcome and would be forgiven and have a new life in Messiah. Heaven rejoiced to see the Golden Urn on the Mercy Seat in the holy of holies. It would forever be heaven's most glorious centerpiece! Cover the mercy seat with the Lamb's blood, check!

"For we do not have a high priest who is unable to empathize with our weaknesses, but we have one who has been tempted in every way, just as we are yet he did not sin." (Hebrews 4:15)

Back in Jerusalem the faithful were grieving. Their Rabbi was gone, taken so unfairly. They were afraid, hiding in a room wondering want to do next. I knew it was time to bring the Risen One back to Jerusalem to finish the mission, so off we shot.

In our absence the disciples had gathered together with doors locked for fear of the ones who had killed their leader. Now Jesus stepped into their midst with joy, love and compassion to reassure them their Messiah lived. Peace be with you! They could hardly believe their eyes and one disciple even had to touch the place in Jesus' side where the sword had pierced him to be convinced.

The joy of the reunion! During the next forty days Jesus visited his followers, shared meals with them and provided tips on finding

fish. Finally, he blew his breath out upon his friends and gave them the gift of the Holy Spirit to fill, empower and go forward in victory. He had overcome the world and now they would share the light of that message with a world desperately struggling in darkness!"

Then it was over, time to go. I thought of the Father and how pleased he must be that his daring plan with his son had succeeded. The greatest story ever told, and I, Gabriel, am his witness. Ascension into heaven, check! Mission accomplished, check!

The Shelf

The magic of Hawaii loomed larger than life as we made preparations for our long-awaited vacation. Now finally in Maui, an island filled with beauty, we sat back, breathed deeply of the tropical air, and relaxed. Let the trade winds blow!

After walking on the beach, taking photos of the amazing blue ocean and watching vacationers body surf, it was time to venture out and explore. We headed to a nearby plaza to see the sights, engage in retail therapy, and happy hour. People were everywhere, going in and out, making purchases and juggling bags. And right there in the midst of the island heat, summer breeze, and happy shoppers, an image floated by me. A simple brush stroke of brown across the faces and backs of nearby pedestrians, teasing me to look.

Earlier that day, I had pondered something my pastor had said in a recent sermon. He had mentioned that the end times started with the life of Jesus and would continue until his return. I was happy to hear that, so I didn't have to wonder when the end times would begin. They were already here! An odd thing to think about on vacation, but soon I would understand.

Everywhere I looked, there it was. Just a horizontal stroke of brown over the ocean, across the trees. I tried to put the image out of my mind but could not, for it was a puzzle begging to be solved. We finished our shopping and headed for home.

That evening as we sat on the sand enjoying the sunset and a bottle of wine, the brown s t r o k e continued to float a few feet away. I could almost reach out and touch it. The

image hung in the air and beckoned me to come closer. Why was this image haunting me and for what purpose? Then I heard the whisper, "Create a display shelf befitting a carpenter and king."

Now I knew the game was afoot, so I picked up my spiritual paintbrush and jumped in! Narnia, here we go! First a rainbow to set the stage. A line here, a stroke there, step back and look. Too light? Too dark? Is this a horizontal shelf or a vertical book case?

As I dabbed and stroked, I decided it was a single shelf and spanned a long distance. Like a bracelet encircling the wrist, or a shelf encircling the globe. So, what is going on the shelf? I added brown leather-bound albums, one for each year of Jesus' life up to the present time. I mixed red paint and splashed on crimson, the color of blood and life.

Then at either end of the long wooden shelf blocks appeared. At first the blocks looked like rectangles but then they transformed into cylinders. They were to become impressive bookends. This was a special shelf created to represent the reign of Jesus from his birth to his return.

I considered the cylinders destined to become bookends. I looked at them and imagined different scenarios then made my decisions and carved the images into the wood. The Alpha bookend was engraved with the star of Bethlehem, the nativity scene, Jesus the carpenter, Jesus the rabbi with his disciples, the cross, the empty tomb, and then Jesus rising up into the clouds. On top of this cylinder was a small statue of The Lamb, power controlled. One could rotate it to view the images. This was the story of his first visit and commitment to the defeat of sin and death.

The Omega bookend was engraved with Jesus on a white horse leaping through heaven's gate, horse and rider one, bent low, hair, mane, and tail streaming behind; legions of heaven's warriors following in hot pursuit with a great cloud of witness; the sword, which is the word of God and then Jesus's descent onto the Mount of Olives with the ground cleft under his feet. On top of this cylinder was the Lion, power unleashed, that could be rotated as well. This was the story of his second visit and commitment to reclaim planet earth for his glory.

The shelf stretched the span of the end times from the beginning to the end. Each album held a collection of people and events, in the order of their occurrence, that were close to the heart of Jesus. Abraham Lincoln,

Martin Luther King Jr., Billy Graham, and Mother Theresa, people who had made a difference for his kingdom. But most importantly the albums contained the photos and names of all the ordinary people who had placed their faith in him. I put gold numbers on the spine of each album according to the year it represented. Beneath the shelf I placed a sign, *The Lamb's Book of Life*. The book's name was painted in gold-leaf, for the names it contained were precious. His living words were painted in vermillion red for his atoning blood.

"I give them eternal life, and they shall never perish; no one will snatch them out of my hand. My Father, who has given them to me, is greater than all; no one can snatch them out of my Father's hand. I and the Father are one." (John 10:29)

Then I stepped back, surveyed the scene, and it was finished. A shelf of great honor created to display the ultimate prize, the Lamb's beautiful bride! How perfect, I could just see angels at the gates of heaven placing leis around the necks of believers as they entered the pearly gates. It would be a marriage made in paradise, indeed!

In this perfect paradise the King's family album is on display for all eternity. We will be able go to the brown wooden shelf and select the album of our time and find our face and name in it! And if we look really close, we just might see orchids, sunsets, blue skies, and ocean spray imprinted on the pages. What a marvelous Hawaiian adventure!

"Let us rejoice and be glad and give the glory to Him, for the marriage of the Lamb has come and His bride has made herself ready. And it was given to her to clothe herself in fine linen, bright and clean; for the fine linen is the righteous acts of the saints. And he said to me, Write, blessed are those who are invited to the marriage supper of the Lamb. And he said to me, these are true words of God." (Revelation 19:7–9)

The Partner

Books are written on this subject. "What is a partner?" "How does one find a partner?" and "How does one be a good partner?" The world has many opinions, but my thoughts are not on these questions. As you know by now, this book is about Jesus. Never in my life did I purpose to write a book, and certainly not one about Jesus Christ of Nazareth, but here we are. This is his book, and he has prompted me to share an important point, which is that *he loves you*!

The partnership to discuss here is that of marriage. Not an earthly marriage/partnership forged in our natural realm, but a marriage/partnership yet to take place in the paradise. The marriage of Jesus and each individual who has said "yes" to him. People known collectively as the church or the body of Christ.

An earthy marriage contract can be decided on by two sets of parents, who arrange a marriage, hoping to establish a good match. Or it can be decided on by two individuals who, for many reasons, decide to take the plunge. There are always two parties of decision-making people that arrive at a conclusion. Good match? Or bad match?

With Jesus, it is different. He has already chosen us, even before the foundation of the earth. No two-party system. No courtship dances of back and forth, *Maybe I will, maybe I won't, maybe I can do better.* Jesus is constant, standing solid in place, waiting. His mind is made up. All the indecision, moving forward, then backward, are on our side. Jesus just stands at the door and knocks. Tap, tap, tap. Then one day we get up our courage and open the door. Jesus is standing there. He kneels down, looks up into our eyes and says, "I love you, may I come into your heart and will you be my bride?" This is our chance and when we say, "Yes, Jesus, please come into my heart and teach me about you," he steps through the door, into our heart, and gives us his pledge of the Holy Spirit. His engagement ring to declare that we are his. Jesus will never leave us nor forsake us, he has sealed the deal.

> *"Now it is God who establishes both us and you in Christ. He anointed us, set his seal of ownership on us, and put his Spirit in our hearts as a deposit, guaranteeing what is to come." (2 Corinthians 1:21–22)*

Now the partnership begins. We fall in love with our betrothed and get to know him. What is he like, what pleases him? Jesus continues to woo us and teach us about himself. In the process we change and transform into his beautiful bride. The bride he fell in love with from before the foundation of the earth. This may sound like fantasy, but I promise you the day will come when we stand before him and it is *real!* God created marriage on earth to reflect Jesus's relationship with the church. Being imperfect humans, and living in a fallen world, we often don't experience marriage the way it was intended to be. The following is a scripture describing God's view point of an ideal marriage.

> *"Husbands, love your wives, just as Christ loved the church and gave himself up for her to make her holy, cleansing her by the washing with water*

through the word, and to present her to himself as a radiant church, without stain or wrinkle or any other blemish, but holy and blameless. In this same way, husbands ought to love their wives as their own bodies. He who loves his wife loves himself. After all, no one ever hated their own body, but they feed and care for their body, just as Christ does the church—for we are members of his body. "For this reason a man will leave his father and mother and be united to his wife, and the two will become one flesh." This is a profound mystery—but I am talking about Christ and the church. However, each one of you also must love his wife as he loves himself, and the wife must respect her husband." (Ephesians 5:25-33, NIV)

Jesus is our intended soul mate, and we are his intended bride. Someday we will look into his eyes and experience a perfect love, perfect union, and perfect completion but only if we have said *yes* to his knock. This is a relationship that only God could have planned. Jesus, our perfect partner, is waiting, and he *"wants all people to be saved and to come to a knowledge of the truth." (1 Timothy 2:4)*

Come to the Paradise!

You are cordially invited to attend the

Marriage supper of
the Lamb and his Beautiful Bride

The ceremony will be a lavish feast held in the sacred banquet halls of heaven. Attending will be myriads of angels rejoicing with the bridal party! The date is to be determined.

Please reply in order to have your name inscribed on the guest list. Only those with names recorded will be granted entrance. This invitation will expire on the day of your departure from earth or the day of the Lord's return.

____ Yes, I will attend for my name is already on the guest list.
____ Yes, I accept the invitation of salvation with joy, skepticism, fear and excitement. Jesus please come into my heart and cover my sins with your sacrifice of love. I want to come to the greatest party ever known!

Standing by are angels ready to receive your answer with trumpets raised ready to celebrate your decision!

Don't delay for today is the day of salvation!

Heaven's Gate

How exciting it was to receive the beautiful, engraved invitation in the mail! The *most* wonderful event in history, and I was on the guest list! I checked the space, placed the response in the envelope, and sealed it. The response envelope was addressed to: "Special Delivery, Heaven's Gate"

Hmm, that's interesting. The scent of fragrant tropical flowers suddenly seemed to fill the room. Then I saw her standing there, in a portal framed with flowers, holding blossoms out to me.

"I was sent to collect your response and take it back to heaven's gate. We don't want to delay in recording your name on the guest list!" I couldn't speak, only watch the beautiful angel as she took my envelope and said, *"Come to the Paradise with me for a moment and take a peek!"* She took my hand, and I stepped through the portal . . . onto a platform, looking up at a huge gate of pearl, brilliant and shining. *"Come on, here is the Special Delivery box, put your letter in, and let's go!"*

That was the beginning of my visit to Eden North, aka the Paradise! Wow, I was so excited to be there and with the special escort of an angel! *"My name is Iris and I am a flower angel. It is such a dreamy job, I love bringing touches of color and fragrance to the sons of man. Ministering to their needs is very important to the Master and I want to please him in every way."* Iris pushed the gate open, beckoned for me to follow, and we stepped into the glorious kingdom.

She held her finger to her lips to silence me, *"Now, this is just a quick peek, and I know you will want to stay, but just remember, it is not your time yet."* And then a quick wink as she took my hand.

I found myself holding on to the tip of a white, feathered wing as we jetted up and away. Looking back, it would remind me of Peter Pan, but now all I wanted to do was take in the experience of bliss!

Below us was a perfect garden, colorful, orderly, trimmed, and luscious. That was the description that I could apply to everything I saw. Along with an abundance of flowers in every color imaginable, were trees with ripe fruit, paths of soft green grass, rainbow hued birds, brilliant blue sky, and everywhere the most glorious music! Choirs of angels sang words 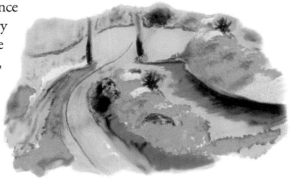 and melodies that defy earthly sound. Every note was perfect, enriching and adding to the glory of heaven and the Master.

Below us in the garden, walking on the paths, were the sons of man. They were a beautiful sight to behold! Happy, chatting, friends, and family strolling in harmony. Some had dogs, and others had small children with them. I didn't know their nationalities, couldn't hear their language, or determine what they were sharing. All were dressed in soft white robes that flowed around their bodies, and they looked comfortable. Soon we were flying over a city with tall buildings that looked like they meant business. The buildings were made of marble and had magnificent carvings announcing their purpose. Jewels embedded on the walls sparkled and added to the brilliance of the display. On we went, circling over what resembled a large entertainment venue. We descended and landed softly on a hill opposite the large stage.

Everywhere I looked were people, but not like we have in our realm. These people were all in good health and their ages varied from very young to mid-prime. They seemed to be from all ethnic groups. There were no crutches, wheelchairs, walkers, oxygen tanks, caregivers, or infirmity. Everyone was whole, healthy, intact, connected, relaxed, happy, and beautiful. All were on the same team with the same goals and values. Their faces glowed with contentment.

Iris bent low and whispered to me, *"This area is called the Heavenly Bowl and is devoted to what on earth might be called an Open Mic Night or Improvisation. Anyone can get up and tell their*

story of how the Master worked in their life and set them free. How they got on Heaven's Guest List. Here we glorify the Master continually and the stories are always wonderful! We also have the most glorious musicians from among the sons of man who accompany the stories and contribute their talent given to them by the Master. Oh, and the actors, don't get me started! They have all of us in stitches laughing, tears, applause, and hanging on every word . . . Sometimes we have to come back to see the next performance to find out how the story ended . . . Let's get going before our time is up, and I have to get back to work. Hang on!"

Next, I found myself on top of a beautiful mountain that overlooked the garden, tall buildings and Heavenly Bowl.

"There are many more parts to the realm, but those will be for another time. I've taken you to this mountain because in this kingdom mountains are wonderful! They aren't obstacles to be cast into the sea. Instead they are for loveliness, adventure and picnics. The citizens of heaven can travel anywhere they want and enjoy recreation, fellowship, and even challenge themselves to new heights. Like climbing this mountain for instance!"

We spent a moment admiring the view and then we were off to our next stop. I wasn't sure what it would be but was pleasantly surprised to land before a large gold double-door and smell the wonderful aroma of food being prepared!

"This way," Iris whispered. *"This is Eden's Kitchen, famous for the most wonderful delicacies that you can imagine. Everything is made with love and the master angel-chef is preparing for the Big Event. We are all looking forward to celebrating the Lamb and his Bride!"*

Iris pushed the door open a crack, and I could see the activity of many angels stirring, chopping, arranging, counting, folding, whipping, and any other function that happens when a banquet is being prepared. The images and the aroma were overwhelming and I absolutely did not want to go back. How unfair to have to wait for all the joys of heaven.

"Come, we must go," she said and took my hand. I stepped through the pearly gates, onto the platform, through the portal and was back in my familiar surroundings. Iris waved her fingers and said, *"I can't wait to see you again when we don't have to say good-bye . . ."* And then she was gone. The fragrance of the flowers lingered as I tried to make sense of this amazing adventure. So sweet, so wonderful, so short. Thank you, Iris, for giving me a glimpse of heaven!

Every Ear Shall Hear

During the process of developing this book, Erika, Crowned One, and I had discussions about blessings that might possibly result from our efforts. We were happy to be progressing with God's stories and illustrations and excited to see where it would go once we were finished. Then God weighed in and gave me his perspective. Just a few words, *"Every ear shall hear . . ."* I wasn't sure what those words meant, but I knew they were powerful. I looked them up and found this scripture:

> *"And this gospel of the kingdom will be preached in the whole world as a testimony to all nations, and then the end will come." (Matthew 24:14)*

God had spoken. This book was inspired by the Holy Spirit to continue the presentation of the good news, the great commission, given to his followers over two thousand years ago:

> *"All authority in heaven and on earth has been given to me. Go therefore and make disciples of all nations, baptizing them in the name of the Father and of the Son and of the Holy Spirit, teaching them to observe all that I have commanded you. And behold, I am with you always, to the end of the age." (Matthew 28:18–20)*

> *"The Lord is not slow in keeping his promise, as some understand slowness. Instead he is patient with*

*you, not wanting anyone to perish, but everyone to
come to repentance." (2 Peter 3:9)*

*"Trust in the LORD forever, for the LORD, the
LORD himself, is the Rock eternal." (Isaiah 26:4)*

This is his greatest desire! May the King's Jewels sparkle, shine
and glow in our hearts. May every ear hear, and may his plan be
accomplished according to his purpose. Amen!

When I first heard the call to write down these stories, I thought
it was my idea. It was fun and the stories popped in my head like
corn popping at the movie theater. As I progressed in the writing, I
saw this project as a pyramid that originated with me at the top. I
wondered how it would all come together and then the Lord spoke
to me: *"There is a pyramid but you have the order wrong. I am the one
with the vision and the one who is orchestrating this project. I am the
apex and below me are the team members for peace, beauty, and joy. Each
member has a connecting line up to me, and there is a connecting line
between each member at the bottom of the pyramid. The members are
first joined to me and then to each other. This model can accommodate
as many members as I choose to call."*

That was wonderful to hear, and I had a good laugh at myself!
Now I understood that God was the originator and organizer, and
I was just lucky to be called to be part of it. So, God brought the
stories to mind, and I typed them. Even though they were my life
experiences, the messages, rocks, lessons, and gems are all his. During
the writing, I sometimes wondered what my next step would be,
where I would take this book. *Where will it go, how will it go and who
will it touch?*

Of course, I got a reply, and naturally one that I wasn't
expecting. *"It isn't where you take the book, it is where the book takes
you."* God is always simple and direct. I thought about it and realized
the wonderful places this book has already taken me. I have been
refreshed with learning experiences from the past. I have visited
heaven, seen the gates of hell, experienced True North, heard the
voice of Jesus, hovered with Gabriel over Calvary, beheld a win-win

shield, explored the importance of a name, followed a magic shelf, revisited my shell collection, and glimpsed paradise!

I am truly blessed that God called me to this project and I have loved every minute of being his typist. I hope it takes you to wonderful places and that you have enjoyed the beautiful illustrations created by Crowned One, Stefan R. Sanford. Thank you for sharing stories of rocks that, under pressure and polishing, became gems. Thank you for sharing my reverie of musings and ponderings. Paradise awaits!

About the Author

Serena Bella, also known as Shelly Boulet, was born and raised in Southern California, and lives in a beachside community with her husband, son, and dogs. She has enjoyed careers in both clothing design and health care administration.

Serena cherishes her family and her family's history, which is filled with teachers, artists, and writers. Design holds a special place in Serena's heart, and she enjoys bringing that process into all areas of her life.

Favorite pastimes have included photography, interior design, collecting beautiful things, and sharing her home with others. Most recently Serena has discovered the love of writing, and hopes to continue creating Peace and Beauty for everyone.

About the Illustrator

Stefan Russell Sanford is a graphic designer and illustrator who has been passionate about art from the time he could hold a pencil. Stefan studied Design Communication Art through the University of Southern California, UCLA and the University of Massachusetts, Amherst. In addition to painting and illustrating, Stefan designs original book covers, movie and play posters, as well as music CD covers. Stefan works with clients in designing graphic labels, branding, and logos.

Stefan Russell considers *Peace, Beauty, and Joy: Come to the Paradise!* a pathway to knowing the lordship of Jesus Christ and considers his art to be a gift from God.